Cultural Ecstasies

In this important contribution to the field, Ilana Mountian critically analyses discourses surrounding drugs, addiction, drug prohibition, treatment and prevention, and highlights new ways of understanding the role that gender plays in the ethics of drug use across cultures.

The book analyses the discourses of religion, criminality and medicine, and shows how they, combined with key historical events, affect our views of drug use and drug users based on gender, race and class.

The book draws on research from a variety of fields to provide alternative conceptual and methodological perspectives on the subject, including:

- critical theory
- gender studies
- post-colonial studies
- psychoanalysis
- philosophy.

Cultural Ecstasies is an innovative study of drugs and addiction, and will be of great interest to students, researchers and professionals working in psychology, sociology, social work, health care, criminology, and allied disciplines. This book draws on critical theories, discourse analysis and Lacanian psychoanalysis to provide theoretical frameworks for critical analysis and to investigate and rework the predominant concepts in the fields of drugs and gender.

Ilana Mountian is an Honorary Research Fellow and a member of the Discourse Unit at Manchester Metropolitan University, UK. She also holds a postdoctoral research position at the Universidade de São Paulo, Brazil. Her research practice involves the application of interdisciplinary perspectives, including critical theories, gender studies, post-colonial studies and psychoanalysis, to the study of drug use, immigration and gender.

Concepts for Critical Psychology: Disciplinary Boundaries Re-thought
Series editor: Ian Parker

Developments inside psychology that question the history of the discipline and the way it functions in society have led many psychologists to look outside the discipline for new ideas. This series draws on cutting edge critiques from just outside psychology in order to complement and question critical arguments emerging inside. The authors provide new perspectives on subjectivity from disciplinary debates and cultural phenomena adjacent to traditional studies of the individual.

The books in the series are useful for advanced level undergraduate and postgraduate students, researchers and lecturers in psychology and other related disciplines such as cultural studies, geography, literary theory, philosophy, psychotherapy, social work and sociology.

Published Titles:

Surviving Identity
Vulnerability and the Psychology of Recognition
By Kenneth McLaughlin

Psychologisation in Times of Globalisation
By Jan De Vos

Social Identity in Question
Construction, Subjectivity and Critique
By Parisa Dashtipour

Cultural Ecstasies
Drugs, Gender and the Social Imaginary
By Ilana Mountian

Forthcoming Titles:

Ethics and Psychology
Beyond Codes of Practice
By Calum Neill

Self Research
The Intersection of Therapy and Research
By Ian Law

Cultural Ecstasies

Drugs, gender and the social imaginary

Ilana Mountian

Routledge
Taylor & Francis Group
LONDON AND NEW YORK

First published 2013
by Routledge
4 Park Square, Milton Park, Abingdon, Oxon OX14 4RN
605 Third Avenue, New York, NY 10017

Routledge is an imprint of the Taylor & Francis Group, an informa business

British Library Cataloguing in Publication Data
A catalogue record for this book is available from the British Library

Library of Congress Cataloging-in-Publication Data
Mountian, Ilana.
Cultural ecstasies: drugs, gender and the social imaginary/
Ilana Mountian.
p. cm.
Includes bibliographical references.
1. Drug abuse – Social aspects. 2. Drug addiction – Social aspects.
3. Women – Drug use. 4. Women drug addicts. I. Title.
HV5801.M68 2012
362.29 – dc23 2012012677

ISBN 13: 978-0-415-58383-1 (hbk)
ISBN 13: 978-0-415-58386-2 (pbk)
ISBN 13: 978-0-203-09659-8 (ebk)

Typeset in Times New Roman
by Florence Production Ltd, Stoodleigh, Devon

For my family and friends

Contents

Acknowledgements

I would like first to thank Ian Parker for including this book in the series and I am grateful to Erica Burman and Ian Parker for their friendship and appreciated contributions to this work.

I would also like to thank Routledge and its publishing team, Christine Horrocks and the other two reviewers for their comments and suggestions for this publication; Manchester Metropolitan University for the opportunity of developing this work; the Discourse Unit, the Feminist Research and Reading Group and the PRODOC/CAPES programme for their support.

For my friends and colleagues who supported and contributed to this work: Ángel Gordo-López, Khatidja Chantler, Calum Neill, Marco Aurélio Máximo Prado, Miriam Debieux, Christian Dunker, Ana Paula Gianesi, Monica Londoño, Viviani Catroli, Elena Calvo Gonzalez, Mihalis Mentinis, Daniela Mountian and André Gal Mountian.

1 Introduction

Taking a critical psychological approach, this deconstructionist account explores and informs elements of the social imaginary of drugs and gender, and intersections with sexuality, race, class and age. The analysis highlights the often contradictory and ambiguous definitions of drugs and addiction, and how these relate to broader ethical and moral concerns. This book is primarily a critical analysis on the theme of drugs and gender; by generating a wider field for debate, it contributes to more progressive social policies, highlighting key aspects to be taken in account in research.

This book aims first to provide theoretical frameworks for critical analysis and second to highlight critical insights into mainstream discourses on drugs, addiction and drugs users. For this aim, examples drawing on the history of drugs, drug treatment and drug policies will be utilised. Seen as social text, these will serve to highlight underlying key discursive foundations. Analysis of gender will work in two ways: I utilise gender as a means for deconstructing drugs and to unravel effects of drug discourses on gender. It is claimed that understandings of drugs, drug treatment and drug policies have to be seen in their specific social and political contexts; therefore I do not provide ready-made answers to these viewpoints. Instead, I offer, on the one hand, an approach to deconstruct and build alternative discourses in this area, while, on the other hand, I call attention to key aspects in the fields of drugs that are often excluded in both conceptualisations of drugs and drug policies, such as gender and intersections with sexuality, class, race and age.

This approach is partly the result of my previous research undertaken in England (Mountian, 1999, 2004a, 2005b) and my clinical practice in the area of drug treatment. As a clinical psychologist in Brazil and given my experience as a visiting clinical psychologist in England and in France, I had witnessed the struggles of the drug addict and the wide range of procedures and explanations for addiction. Furthermore, I was puzzled by how societal views on this issue inform the use of drugs and contribute to define and maintain certain forms of identifications (of the addict, for example). I felt the need for critical perspectives to contrast with (which typically seemed restricted to) medical, legal and/or moralistic approaches.

By giving examples of discourses of a range of drugs, and in diverse contexts, I highlight how approaches to drugs appear in many instances individualistic, reductionist, self-evident and contradictory, and how these discourses are frequently polarised, oscillating between only good or bad, and often informed and produced by moral panics. Of course, I am also not ignoring the different effects of different drugs, as well as the quantity and frequency of use of subjects, but rather I am emphasising the societal views of specific uses of drugs. Further, in terms of drug treatment, the clinical practice indicates that each case should be seen individually, accounting for their social context.

In order to produce this critical account, I utilise contributions from critical psychology, critical theories, gender studies, feminist research, queer studies, post-colonial studies, philosophy and psychoanalysis. Philosophical perspectives and psychoanalytical notions are used in various ways in this book. Their main contribution is to provide the means for deconstructing taken-for-granted assumptions, bringing different perspectives to these debates. The encounter with gender perspectives and post-colonial studies provides both a theoretical background for a political agenda concerned with power inequalities, and to the role of deconstruction and challenge of naturalising and dominating categories in discourse. These include sexuality, race, class and age.

The classification of drugs as established by the World Health Organization includes all psychoactive substances, legal and illegal (tobacco, alcohol, anti-depressives, tranquillisers, amphetamines, marijuana, heroin, cocaine, etc.). Hence, in this book you will not find an emphasis on a specific drug, although some drugs are more discussed than others. Rather, I juxtapose different approaches to what is discursively stipulated as drugs in order to highlight how the cultural, social and political contexts define drugs. For example, alcohol is shown to have a variety of usages and meanings: as a recreational drug, medicine, food and sacred substance. This work draws on broad mainstream discourses of drugs in Western societies. It does not claim to generalise or restrict discourses of drugs, to those identified, but rather it highlights key discourses and their effects.

The definition of gender needs also to be clarified. Gender is not understood as a natural and biological predisposition, but rather as a performative process (Butler, 1993), in terms of what is socially expected from gender categories. This approach can be extended to address other power relationships, such as those surrounding race, age and class differences. In this book, although the main focus is on women, the categories identified should not be read as women's categories, in the sense of being properties of women.

This deconstruction of discourses on drugs and gender therefore challenges essentialist approaches to what is understood as natural and/or moral categorisations. Moreover, taking gender into account provides two main resources for analysis: on the one hand, it allows us to look at how gender figures in the field of drugs and, on the other hand, understanding gender as a place of inequality broadens the discussion to include analysis of power relations within contemporary cultural-political practices.

The focus on the notion of the 'social imaginary' is used in this book to emphasise the importance of images, fantasies, desires, ideas and (mis)recognition, to the constitution of subjectivity. Although I am emphasising the importance of these aspects to the constitution of subjectivity, it is crucial to highlight that at no point is the individual (nor the notion of subjectivity) understood as separate from society, society in the radical sense, including language, history, culture, etc. Rather, the individual is intrinsically social.

The notion of the other will be employed in the analysis of drugs and drug users based on two main theoretical approaches: the Foucauldian tradition on otherness and Lacanian psychoanalytic insights into the imaginary other and the symbolic big Other. This work is also illustrated by an analysis of visual images in media and interviews from previous research.

The discursive object 'drug' is explored in this book as condensing a wide area of investigation, related to religious, medical, judicial, economic, political and cultural realms. Mainstream discourses on drugs are often situated in the interplay between medical and religious discourses, and consequent legislative imperatives, thereby allowing us to unravel ethical and moral aspects in which these discourses are embedded. Throughout this book, examples are given in order to illuminate and counter existing mainstream discourses, as a device to generate further debate. Although I do not provide prompt prescriptive answers to the questions raised within this book, I focus attention on the imaginary formations of drugs, drug users and gender as aspects that are typically overlooked. I believe these are vital aspects to be taken into consideration, since they also inform drug legislation and practices (e.g. forms of intoxication). Hence, this book offers a contribution towards mapping the way in which these aspects have been worked through, providing insights into drug policies.

The book is divided into seven chapters. Chapter 2 sets the conceptual frameworks for critical psychology and to the deconstruction proposed, that is, the notions of social imaginary and discourse and contributions from feminist research, queer studies and post-colonial studies. In Chapter 3, in order to contextualise the often-contrasting debates around drugs, key historical events are highlighted, providing insights into the meanings and social functions of drugs. It is important to note that the aim is not to trace a genealogy of drugs, but rather to highlight key discourses that provide the ground for the following analysis of the moral and ethical standpoints of health and drugs, focusing on the interplay of the racialised, classed and sexualised gendered formation of drugs and drug users.

These discourses can be seen in circulation in most Western countries, having similar discursive constructions (medical, religious and legislative discourses). I concentrate particularly on the UK and US history of drugs, as these have a major impact in policies worldwide, particularly on prohibition. The discourses highlighted in the book point to key aspects to be considered in future studies in this field, that is, the impact of religious, medical, political discourses, and the need to consider gender, sexuality, class and race, as well as the social and cultural contexts and consequent specificities of drug use for drug policies.

In Chapter 4, I critically analyse current definitions of drugs and addiction, attending both to their antagonistic definitions and the moral foundations of mainstream medical discourses. Two main aspects are emphasised here: specific understandings of 'health' and morality (Katz, 1997), and the production of hierarchical moral dichotomies within drug discourses, such as good and bad, natural and artificial, true and false, and accounting for the importance of classifying drugs as legal and illegal as defining the modern era of drug use (Xiberras, 1989). Here, I elaborate on the flexible notion of *Pharmakon* (as both remedy and poison, Derrida, 1997) and explore the notion of free will within drug discourses (Sedgwick, 1992).

Chapter 5, 'Drug use and social imaginary', addresses some of the aspects of the imaginary surrounding the drug user, which often circulate around the victim and the threat in discourse, drawing on Badiou's (2001) analysis of ethics and the relation to 'difference', and on Foucault's (1991) works on mechanisms of power and the formation of the other, I highlight aspects of the moral background of the war on drugs.

Chapter 6 concentrates on discourses of the female drug user. The categories of victim and threat and the notion of the other are analysed as being transposed on to the feminine, whereby discourses on drug use around weakness, uncontrollability, madness and dependency are highlighted, notions also typically feminised. From these perspectives, I analyse some visual images of women and drugs.

Moreover, I present an analysis of the association between women and drugs in which 'sexual vulnerability' and the relation with race figures in discourse. Here, the idea of nation plays an important role, in which women are posited as symbolically representing and reproducing nation (Yuval-Davis, 1997). Hence, the imaginary formation of the 'public woman vs. woman in public' (Kohn, 1992) has specific effects in relation to this field, being intrinsically related to the dynamics of (in)visibility (Ettorre, 1989). There are three aspects to this dynamic: women as being more visible (in relation to the social gaze), invisible women (e.g. drinking at home, medical drugs) (Littlewood, 1994; Ettorre and Riska, 1995), and how paradoxically this visibility produced the conditions for women's use of drugs, seen at times as challenging social stereotypical roles. This social gaze is seen as highly sexualised, where discourses often circulate around the mother or mother-to-be (victim, childlike, innocent, bad mother) (asexual), prostitute (hypersexual) or homosexual.

In Chapter 7, I briefly discuss the impact of this specific social imaginary into drug policies, which often oscillate between punishment and treatment. I highlight the lack of research and treatment that take gender and sexuality as relevant, and the problems associated when punitive models are applied (e.g. losing guardianship of children, sterilisation – also for men in this case).

It is important to point out that the main objective of this book is to critically analyse mainstream discourses on drugs, unravelling ideological, moral and ethical values of these discourses. It aims to provide a broader analysis of the current debates on drug use that seem all too often to be framed by a moralistic standpoint that is presumed and unquestioned, and so uncontested and naturalised. In such a complex and controversial field, major intellectual and political manoeuvres are frequently required in order to escape subscribing to moralistic approaches such as good or bad, for such commitments to value judgements tend to foreclose the available range of analysis. Thus,

I want to make clear that I do not ignore the suffering of the drug user, the circularity of addiction or the damage caused by some forms of intoxicationm but by situating these contemporary phenomena within their social climates and contexts, we can begin to reassess practical and policy approaches that avoid the widespread psychological stigmatisation and demonisation of drug users.

2 Conceptualising the social imaginary

Setting the theoretical ground

This book offers a critical approach to mainstream discourses on drugs, underlying discursive structures of societal practices, and locates the roles of discourses on drugs within these. This, then, is primarily a critical psychological work, in which I set to analyse societal discursive foundations, metaphysical dichotomies, ideological, moral and ethical standpoints, and so forth. A key claim of this book is that discourses on drugs reveal specific societal moral values and ethical standpoints.

By offering a critical approach to discourses on drugs, focusing on the social imaginary of drugs and its intersections with gender perspectives, contributions from different perspectives are required in order to access the different meanings and practices. In the drug field, there are a large number of academic approaches within this range. The book focuses mainly on the critical deconstruction of medical, sociological and psychological research. Douglas (1987), discussing anthropological research on alcohol, argues that anthropological approaches do not necessarily treat drinking as a problem, and this contrasts with the work of specialists in alcohol abuse who focus upon pathology, 'their assumptions and methods are problem-oriented'. One of the effects of this kind of approach is that it can produce an exaggeration, which is evidenced by critical research (Douglas, 1987). This approach often produces individualistic analysis, risking pathologising the subject, and, by decontextualising drug use from society, it does not consider social structural imbalances, reproducing these very social dynamics, and maintaining the invisibility of specific groups (e.g. women, Ettorre and Riska, 1995). From this, it becomes clear that research on drugs is not value-free, but rather it expresses political and moral standpoints prevalent within this area.

Attempting to avoid individualising and/or pathologising approaches, this book proposes a debate on discourses on drugs and their transformations throughout history, treating the material as social text, including images available in the broad media and interviews from previous research (Mountian, 1999, 2004a). Visual texts provide important resources for critical analysis (Mountian 2005a, Mountian *et al.*, 2011). Rose (2001) highlights how images are not only a product of the social context, rather they are also productive, having their own effects, (re)producing power relations. Taking into account the work of Barthes (1973) and Saussure (1974), this reading will be primarily based on discourse analytic approaches.

In this chapter, I present the main theoretical perspectives and epistemological background for this analysis, aiming to unravel understandings of meaning production, following a deconstructionist approach. I draw on a variety of contributions, including the fields of history (Berridge and Edwards, 1987; Escohotado, 1998; Musto, 1999), anthropology (Douglas, 1987; McKenna, 1992; MacRae, 1998), social theories (Bourdieu, 1977; Xiberras, 1989; Coomber, 1994, 1998; N. Rose, 1994; Illich, 1995; Klein, 1995) and feminist research on drug use (Kohn, 1992; McDonald, 1994; Ettorre and Riska, 1995; Campbell, 2000).

Epistemological perspectives

Critical research (Foucault, 2002/1969; Teo, 2005) and gender studies (feminist research and queer studies) have made clear that knowledge is not neutral, but rather the contextualisation of the epistemological background is paramount.

Harding (1986) argues on the importance of making explicit the epistemological background and the distinction between method, methodology and epistemology, that is, method relates to the techniques for gathering the research material, a technical device; methodology specifies the theoretical background for how the study should proceed; and epistemology refers to the philosophical perspective that enables to decide the type of possible knowledge and what can be known (e.g. the traditional exclusion of women as 'knowers') (also Maynard, 1994).

In this section, I present some key aspects of the epistemological approach employed in this book, and their methodological implications, and signal how this theoretical approach can be used for critical debates. As a critical psychological enquiry, these theoretical frameworks allow for deconstructing taken-for-granted assumptions, aiming to unravel meanings and significations through exploring social-historical contexts.

Castoriadis (1991) analyses philosophy by taking into account its social-historical location (in this case, focusing on the project of autonomy). He points out that philosophy, by creating self-reflective subjectivity, is a project of breaking closure. Nevertheless, philosophy can break the closure if it retains a gap. This gap does not produce a major break, but rather 'it posits something, reaches results and may as well produce a closure' (ibid.: 21).

This assertion connects with the approach utilised in this book in which, through this process of deconstruction, it aims to open up some 'closures' that mainstream perspectives on drugs evoke (e.g. through their presumed but implicit moral standpoints), and attempts to keep a gap.

In relation to this process of deconstruction of taken-for-granted assumptions, Žižek (1992) gives some insights through debating the hermeneutical perspective, in which *preconceit* (preconceptions) are already there, as 'given'. Žižek highlights how the objective of the hermeneutical perspective is to keep visible the 'contours of a 'frame', a 'horizon' that, by remaining invisible (by eluding the subject's grasp), determines the field of vision. Hence, what can or cannot be seen is given 'through a historically mediated frame of *preconceits*' (ibid.: 15). Žižek reminds us that the term *preconceit*, in this sense, does not refer to a pejorative connotation, but it has a transcendental status; i.e. 'it organises our experience into a meaningful totality' (ibid.: 15). Therefore, in this sense, Žižek continues:

> It involves an irreducible limitation of our vision, but this finitude is in itself ontologically constitutive: the world is open to us only within radical finitude. At this level, the impossibility of metalanguage equals the impossibility of a neutral point of view enabling us to see things 'objectively', 'impartially': there is no view that is not framed by a historically determined horizon of 'preunderstanding'.
>
> (ibid.: 15)

This point is crucial since it positions the subject inside history and it makes clear that there is no 'impartial' account, so, in this way, there is no value-free account on discourses of drugs.

Another important epistemological aspect regards the challenge of the separation between object and subject traditional to human sciences (positivistic sciences). This separation has important implications, including the separation between individual and society, which risks dislocating the individual from historical and social contexts.

Here, rather, the subject is understood as intrinsically social, 'historicality is determining characteristic for *Dasein* in the very basis of its Being' (Heidegger, 1997: 42), and '[the] inquiry into Being [ontico-ontological] is itself characterised by historicality' (ibid.: 42). Heidegger understands being-in-the-world as constitutive of the analytic of *Dasein*. *Dasein*'s being 'must be seen and understood *a priori* as grounded upon that state of Being which we have called "Being-in-the-world"' (ibid.: 78). From this comes Alvesson and Skoldberg's (2000: 80) assertion that 'we are irrevocably merged with our world, already before any conscious reflection'.

This understanding has important epistemological and methodological implications. First, the reading proposed in this book is not based on an epistemology that separates subject and object, individual and society. Second, this enables us to explore meanings and significations rather than taking things for granted, so that, for example, meanings are understood as given in their historical location. Drugs and addiction are therefore understood as related to specific social imaginaries and social practices that are historically situated, producing and performing specific meanings.

Meanings, however, are not to be understood as something 'hidden', but rather they are constitutive of everyday experiences. As Heidegger (1997: 37) highlights:

> We must rather choose such a way of access and such a kind of interpretation that this entity can show itself in itself and from itself. And this means that it is to be shown as it is *proximally and for the most part* – in its average *everydayness*.

Phenomenology and existentialism takes history as the place for meaning creation and action. Von Zuben (1984: 67) points out that 'it is to the world that we have to give the credit for our "condemnation to meaning", not as contemplation or construction of meanings, but as inherent to historical and political action'. Moreover, Wittgenstein (1968) claims that there is nothing hidden, and further, depending on the situation, concepts have different meanings. This applies to the analysis of the different approaches to drugs proposed here. Furthermore, Wittgenstein argues that to understand a word is to understand a rule (ibid.: paragraph 43). In this sense, we could argue that to understand the context of drug use we should look at social practices, attending to the rules that govern understandings of drugs.

Furthermore, the work on the deconstruction of etymology of words can be enlightening, as seen in Heidegger and Lacan's work (Dunker,

1996), and, as such, the etymology of key words will be discussed, seen as relevant to social and political understandings of popular notions such as drugs, addiction and narcotics.

Four main contributions from this philosophical approach are highlighted: the philosophical standpoint of non-separation between society and individuals (being-in-the-world), an epistemological (historical) inquiry, the process of deconstruction (not taking things for granted) and the attention to language and meaning (hermeneutics). These philosophical contributions meet many aspects of contemporary theories, such as discourse analysis and feminist research, as explored in this chapter.

Social imaginary

The notion of social imaginary employed here draws on the imaginary dimension from Lacanian psychoanalysis and some aspects of Castoriadis' own formulation of social imaginary (Mountian, 2009). This focus on social imaginary elements, in this case of drugs and drug users, allows us to map and condense key discursive formations of the reading of the texts.

Imaginary, in a broad sense, refers to images, fantasies, illusions and so forth that are seen as relevant to the constitution of subjectivity. These elements both constitute and are constituted by society. It is interesting to note that the notion of social imaginary here connects with many aspects of discourse analysis, since discourse also includes images, texts and ideas. However, the focus on discourse makes explicit a political position when it highlights power relationships, as we shall see. In this way, understandings of discourses and social imaginaries are put forward in this book in distinct and converging ways to approach addiction, health, drug users and gender.

I will start by briefly introducing some key notions from psychoanalysis regarding the social imaginary. My focus is on the imaginary of Lacan's (1991) psychoanalysis, and the relations between the imaginary, the symbolic and the real dimensions, the mirror stage, and the notion of identification.

The three dimensions elaborated by Lacan (the symbolic, the imaginary and the real) are central to his theory. These dimensions are intermingled, and do not function as separate phenomena. Lacan borrows the phrase 'symbolic function' from Lévi-Strauss, based on the idea 'that the social world is structured by certain laws which regulate kinship relations and the exchange of gifts' (Evans, 1996: 201). The symbolic order is a linguistic dimension, since the basic form of exchange is communication (exchange of words, the gift of speech), and both law and structure in general are unthinkable without language. However, Lacan does not reduce language to the symbolic, as language involves the three dimensions: real, symbolic and imaginary.

The imaginary relates to dual relations and the symbolic consists of a triadic structure that includes the big Other (Chapter 6). Therefore, it is not related to biology, but rather to the real. However, symbols do not come from the real; the real is that which cannot be symbolised – it resists symbolisation.

Lacan identifies how language provides access to the symbolic order, it enables the subject to articulate desire at the same time that it makes experience symbolically mediated, and, as Parker (1997: 187) asserts, 'broken from that which it is supposed to express, that which vanishes into the unconscious as a fantasy space constituted at the very same moment'. Language is organised in the symbolic order constituting the unconscious. It determines subjectivity so that the entrance to the symbolic produces a split between conscious and unconscious. By contrast, the imaginary order produces a unified image, however this unit is illusory, as it is 'both confirmed and sabotaged by language as it opens up a variety of different subject positions' (ibid.: 209).

For Lacan, the imaginary is related to illusion, to identification, narcissism, image, imagination; related to wholeness, duality and similarity. Yet, the imaginary dimension is structured by the symbolic. Hence, in Lacanian theory, the signifier (basic units of language related to structure, words, sounds, acts) is related to the symbolic, and the signified (effect of the signifier and signification that is produced) and signification (meaningfulness, metonymic and metaphoric) to the imaginary. Therefore, it is not possible to approach the imaginary realm without taking into consideration the symbolic networks that structure it. So when I emphasise the imaginary in this book, the aim is to focus on the aspects of identifications, images that are produced within this space of illusion, while, at the same time, it includes the symbolic dimension.

The imaginary develops through the mirror stage. This is not simply a moment in infant development, rather it indicates aspects of the subject's relation to his/her own image (Lacan, 1991). Hence, this stage has an optical representation – it is related to identification, to the changes that occur when the subject assumes an image (*imago*). The function of the mirror stage is related to the function of the imago, 'which is to establish a relation between the organism and its reality – or, as they say, between the *Innenwelt* and the *Unwelt*' (Lacan, 1989: 4).

A further key point that it can be conceptualised is that, when the child enters the symbolic, gender relations are also mapped out, and the fantasies produced by the gaze, at the imaginary level. Developed here is an imaginary position to experience the real. This imaginary mediation, as pointed out by Parker (1997: 219), is constituted by the entry into language, 'into the symbolic order in which there is mediation not only of self-identity but also of the identity of others'. In this sense, the subject's identification is related to the Other, and not an individual developing outside the social.

The key features here are the illusion of completeness that marks the individual's subjectivity and the relationship between the desire of the Other and identification. Thus, desires, fantasies and illusions are fundamental to the constitution of subjectivity. In this way, it is possible to question how imaginary identifications, including gendered identifications, inform types of intoxication. Next, I present further aspects of the notion of the imaginary emphasising the role of misrecognition, discourse and fantasy.

Society and imaginary

From this account, we have established that the subject of psychoanalysis is not conceived within a classic positivist frame, but rather is a subject constituted in language that is already social, through the relation with the 'Other'. The subject, for Lacan, is a linguistic entity and a subject subordinated to the law of the symbolic. Therefore, this conceptualisation breaks with conventional psychological ideas such as self and ego (Macey, 1995). In this way, it is relevant to note how Althusser (1985) utilises psychoanalysis by looking at ideological formations through the domains of the symbolic and the imaginary. The imaginary becomes the source of a theory of ideology (reflections, recognitions and misrecognitions), whereby interpellation provides a structure for an illusory mutual recognition (Macey, 1995). As Žižek (1992: 10) puts it, 'The logic by means of which one (mis)recognises oneself as the addressee of ideological interpellation.'

The social imaginary understood here is therefore related to discourses, images and fantasies, and, drawing on Althusser's reading of psychoanalysis, ideology is already in play, as well as misrecognition.

Rosa (1999a, 2000) highlights the importance of the social imaginary to understand the subjective constitution of the subject, and the relationship between culture and the formation of subjectivity, arguing that the discourse of the 'Other' that is relevant to the constitution of the subject is impregnated by the imaginary production of the social group, that is, it includes fantasies of the social group. The problematic of the subject related to the law, and the law in relation to the subject, is an effect of the way in which social ties (*laços sociais*) are structured, and this is why it is important to look at the fantasies expressed by social groups. Focusing on the history and place occupied by the subject, it is possible to argue that these spaces produce different discourses according to other references, such as social location and gender. Discussing the effects of the social imaginary in street kids, Rosa (1999b) argues that, beyond poverty, there is a social imaginary of delinquency. This example is relevant here, allowing us to ask, beyond the use of drugs, what is the social imaginary evoked for drug users? What are the main discourses that operate within this field?

Attempting to facilitate an investigation of how social fantasies, or imaginary, produce certain discourses, two main aspects are emphasised here in relation to aspects of the social imaginary. First, investigating how possible identifications of the drug user can inform certain processes of intoxication and second, for the analysis of specific imaginaries related to drugs, drugs users and gender that are socially located as (re)producing ideological, ethical and moral values.

The social imaginary in Castoriadis

I briefly introduce here Castoriadis' notion of social imaginary, with emphasis on the imaginary as it relates to signification. Castoriadis (1991: 84) develops the social imaginary in his philosophical inquiry, conceiving of history as creation, that is, 'the creation of total forms of human life'. This self-creation (self-institution) of society is the creation of the human world: things, reality, language, values, norms, that is, 'the creation of the human individual in which the institution of society is massively embedded' (ibid.: 84).

According to Castoriadis' analysis, the social-historical is not created by nature or historical laws, as society is self-created. The *instituting society* is what creates society and history, as opposed to the *instituted society*. This instituting society is the *social imaginary* in the radical sense. Castoriadis points out that what holds society together is its institutions, and institution, in this sense, comprises all the elements, such as language, values, procedures, how to deal with things, and the individual itself and its differentiations, such as men and women, which are given by the society. The social imaginary, therefore, has a fundamental role in the instituting of society.

In his theory, Castoriadis (1986) argues that history is impossible without the productive or creative imagination, or what he calls the *radical imaginary*. The *radical imaginary* 'deploys itself as society and as history: as the social-historical' (1986: 143). And it does so in two realms: the instituting and the instituted. 'The institution is an originary creation of the social-historical field – of the collective-anonymous – transcending, as form (*eidos*), any possible "production" of individuals or of subjectivity' (ibid.: 143).

And, as Castoriadis (1991: 145) emphasises in a later paper, 'Society, *as always already instituted*, is self-creation and capacity for self-alteration. It is the work of the radical imaginary as instituting, which brings itself into being as instituted society as a given, and each time specified, social imaginary.' So, on the one hand, there is the instituting society that is the radical imaginary and, on the other hand, the instituted society that is related to the realm of the social imaginary. Nevertheless, this is not a static formulation, as Castoriadis (1997: 184) points out:

> It is because there is radical imaginary that there is institution: and there can be no radical imaginary except to the extent that it is instituted. It is the circle of the created and the elements of creation: the different elements have to be posited simultaneously.

It is important to emphasise that a fundamental creation of the social imaginary is that they are *signifiable*.

This assertion is fundamental to the understanding of the social imaginary put forward here, aiming to access significations of drugs, drug users and gender; and to explore how these meanings and significations are given, instituted, and at the same time, are instituting.

It is useful here to highlight what Castoriadis (1997) calls the web of meaning the 'magma' of *social imaginary significations*. The institution of society embodies, carries and animates this web. Here, notions such as God, polis, citizen, nation, commodity, money, taboo, virtue, sin, liberty, justice are examples of social imaginary significations. Gender clearly figures among these, as it is given by society, 'beyond sheer anatomical or biological definitions, man, woman, and child are what they are by virtue of the social imaginary significations which make them that' (ibid.: 7). The 'magma' are (an indefinite number of) sets, but are not reducible to them and they cannot be reconstituted 'analytically', as social 'order' or be reduced to mathematical or biological notions of order.

Furthermore, Castoriadis uses the term 'imaginary' because significations involved are not 'rational' or 'real' references only (i.e. they do not correspond to or are not exhausted by), but they are located through a creation. And it is social because they only exist if they are instituted and shared in the anonymous collective. In the imaginary realm, existence is signification. Significations though they can be "pointed to" are not determinate.' They are related to each other through indefinite referral.

Hence, in this book, the focus is on the social imaginary as the range of representations, images and discourses that produce and reproduce meaning. Also, crucially, I attend to the analysis of power structures that participate in the creation of elements of the social imaginary of drugs and drug users.

Discourse

Discourse analysis is not a method or a device in itself, highlighting the importance of discourse in the production of society, it can also be cited as an epistemological resource. As methodology, discourse analysis immediately implies taking into account a historical perspective and discourse as meaning production. Looking at discourses, the aim is to underline the ways in which discourses produce and reproduce meaning. 'Discourses do not simply describe the social world, but categorise it, they bring phenomena into sight' (Parker, 1992: 4).

Foucault's (2002/1969) work is an important theoretical resource for discourse analysis. Foucault provides a theory of the social and its changes, and offers a critical approach to the effects of theory by conceiving theory as a form of discourse (Parker, 2002). Discourse analysis focuses on the 'different ways of structuring areas of knowledge and social practice' (Fairclough, 1992: 3). For example, the medical discourse is the dominant discourse of health care. In this sense, we can already point out that medical discourses are the dominant discourses in the drug field.

Discourses have different manifestations: they reflect, represent, construct and constitute social relationships (constituting key entities and positioning them in different ways) and social practices. A historical perspective, in this way, refers to historical events as contingent. As Kendall and Wickham (1999: 5) point out, 'the emergence of that event was not necessary, but was one possible result of a whole series of complex relations between other events'.

In relation to the methodology derived from discourse analysis, it is important to emphasise that the focus on power relations is central to the analysis. The examination will include the analysis of discontinuities, continuities, what is in the text, what is silenced, contradictions, regularities, differences, repetitions, rules and categories (Foucault, 2002/1969), 'a dialectical reading of texts' (Parker, 2002: 6).

The objective of discourse analysis is not to uncover internal mental states and processes, but to examine how these processes are constructed in discourse (Parker, 2002) and the way concepts operate in practice. For this, a deconstructionist approach is required.

Foucault (2002/1969: 30–31) highlights that, for the analysis of the discursive field:

> We must grasp the statement in the exact specificity of its occurrence, determine its conditions of existence, fix at least its limits, establish its correlations with other statements that may be connected with it, and show what other forms of statements excludes.

This is a crucial assertion for the understanding of discourses on drugs.

Discourse analysis provides a space for critical work in the examination of language and power relationships, identifying dominant discourses historically contextualised. What are the prevalent discourses on drugs? What are the roles of specific discourses? How do they function?

It is relevant here to briefly point out the notions of discourse and power employed in discourse analysis. First, discourse does not refer only to speech, but to the construction of knowledge and social practices, as the entity is a discursive construction. Discourses are constitutive and constituting of structures of knowledge and practice, so, in this sense, discourses are always in transformation. They refer to meanings and significations, to the mechanisms and structures that produce knowledge (power). In the words of Fairclough (1995: 73) 'discourse is shaped by structures, but also contributes to shaping and reshaping them, to reproducing and transforming them'.

Discourses are found in text, and 'texts are delimited tissues of meaning reproduced in *any* form that can be given an interpretative gloss' (Parker, 1992: 6). This follows a way of engaging with Derrida's famous claim: 'There is nothing outside of the text' (Derrida, 1976: 158 in Parker, 1992: 7), while also accounting for how language is productive, that is, discourses produce objects, practices that form the objects of which they speak, including representations, metaphors, images and fantasies. Hence, discourses are productive and performative.

In this sense, it is important to keep in mind that meanings of discourse are not confined to one author or set of intentions. Discourse analysis does not look for something behind the text, but rather it shows how language is constituted independently of one's intention (Parker, 1992). As Burman (2003: 5) points out, 'the purpose of discourse work is not to focus on individuals but rather the cultural frameworks of meaning that they reproduce'. This is an important aspect for the analysis proposed, whereby the aim is not to focus on individuals, but rather to analyse the diverse and often contradictory meanings of drugs that are culturally framed and socially produced.

Hence, the notions of truth and power in Foucault's theory are not related to a universalitisc notion of truth, rather 'truth' is seen 'as a system of ordered procedures for the production, regulation, distribution, circulation and operation of statements' (Rabinow, 1984: 74 in Fairclough, 1992). 'Truth' is related to systems of power, however power is not only related to domination or only to the forms in which power takes place, and it is not a structure or an institution, 'it is the name that one attributes to a complex strategical situation in a particular society' (Foucault, 1998: 93). Power and knowledge in discourse are joined together (ibid.), and power is related to the process, 'the multiplicity of force relations immanent in the sphere in which they operate and which constitute their own organisation' (ibid.: 92). As a process, through struggle, changes and the support these forces have one to another, they constitute a system. Or, on the contrary, they isolate them, appearing as the strategies by which they take place (e.g. state apparatus, law). 'Power's condition of possibility, or in any case the viewpoint which permits one to understand its exercise' (ibid.: 92).

Discourse is 'a series of discontinuous segments whose tactical function is neither uniform nor stable' (ibid: 100). In this way, discourses are not to be read as a world of dominant and dominated discourses, but rather, as Foucault points out, 'as a multiplicity of discursive elements that can come into play in various strategies' (ibid.: 100). The work here is to read this distribution, identifying the variants, including what can be said and what cannot be said, what is expected and what is forbidden, depending on who is speaking, his/her power position and the institutional context. Discourses are not only at the service of power or against it, but rather 'discourses can be both an instrument and an effect of power, but also a hindrance, a stumbling-block, a point of resistance and a starting point for an opposing strategy' (ibid.: 100).

Furthermore, Foucault points out that, at the same time that discourses communicate and produce power, they expose it or make it vulnerable. In this sense, 'silence and secrecy are a shelter for power, anchoring its prohibitions; but they are also loosen its holds and provide for relatively obscure areas of tolerance' (ibid.: 100). Thus, discourse also includes what is censored, what is silenced. As Butler (1997: 133) highlights in relation to censorship, 'censorship seeks to produce subjects according to explicit and implicit norms, and the production of the subject has everything to do with the regulation of speech'.

These aspects indicate an important perspective for this book, whereby the analysis of discourses of drugs and gender requires an elaboration of power relationships, identifying hegemonic discourses and specific ideologies and moral values reproduced, which are socially contextualised.

Feminist research, queer studies and post-colonial studies

Gender studies, and particularly feminist research and queer studies, are employed in this book in two ways: first, in relation to the understanding of gender as performative and not as biological determination, and second, for their contribution to ethical perspectives in research, more specifically to the importance of accounting for power relations in research. These studies combine a number of disciplines, such as, philosophy, epistemology, psychoanalysis and critical theories, in order to deconstruct and challenge mainstream naturalised versions of gender and sex, arguing for the need of situating the politics of research and for the need of political analysis in this field. These traditions influence feminist research in a number of ways relevant to political analysis, including their emphasis on the importance of experience (existentialism), analysis of power relationships (Foucault, 1998), and on debates on psychoanalysis (Stacey, 1993; Gamman and Makinen, 1994; J. Rose,1994; Butler, 1999; Frosh, 1999).

Feminist research highlights some key ethical standpoints for research, which are particularly relevant for this book: attention to groups who are not represented or are misrepresented in research, thereby emphasising categories such as gender, sexuality, class and race (Oakley, 1981; Stanley and Wise, 1990; Harding, 1996; Walkerdine, 1997), and questions related to power and knowledge (Haraway, 1996; Harding, 1996; Longino, 2009), including the power position of the researcher (Oakley, 1981; Burman, 1998; Mountian *et al.*, 2011).

Feminist research, queer studies (Browne and Nash, 2010) and black feminism (hooks, 2000) have a major impact on deconstructing and challenging the apparent neutrality and objectivity of scientific research, challenging the notion of truth as universal, socially locating the subject (man is the universal subject), deconstructing and identifying ideologies under the claim for neutrality (being anti-essentialist) (Burman, 1998), highlighting the importance of situating knowledge (Haraway, 1996) and locating scientific knowledge (Harding, 1986).

This critical epistemological and methodological framework has been of great importance for critical research (Gordo-López and Linaza, 1996; Teo, 2005), and post-colonial studies (McClintock, 1995; Silva *et al.,* 2000; Chantler, 2007; Mountian and Calvo Gonzalez, 2012). In fact, the claim for situated knowledge and intersectionality raises the key importance of understanding gender in relation to its historical and political location, and to consider intersections between sexuality, race, class, age and so forth in the analysis (Spivak, 1988; Anthias and Yuval-Davis, 1996; Burman, 2008; Palmary *et al.,* 2010; Phillips, 2010).

Feminist research analyses the structure of institutions through categories of power. In this way, feminist research is not only concerned with gender inequalities, but with relationships based on power imbalance (class, race, age, sexuality). In this case, my primary focus is on how gender is structured and negotiated within power relationships in patriarchal societies (Benhabib and Cornell, 1987; Pateman, 1988; Moi, 2010).

Hence, it is crucial to highlight imbalances of power in discourse (Foucault, 1998), identifying hegemonic power and how this functions regarding social structures. In this sense, Foucault's work allows us to deconstruct and locate the subject of history, whereby 'classification becomes a form of social categorisation through which what it means to be a subject is defined and regulated in practices during a particular historical period' (Walkerdine, 1997: 23). Power is 'exercised rather than possessed and not primarily repressive, but productive' (Batsleer and Humphries, 2000: 11), that is, it produces subjects; power is an ever-present dynamic that structures interactions in diverse ways (Burman, 1998).

A key conceptualisation, particularly important for queer studies, is related to the understanding of gender not as essentialist or biologically determined, but rather as performative (Butler, 1999). This does not mean that there are not bodies, but rather how bodies perform, and are socially constructed. In this sense, there is no necessary linear, causal (or coherent) relation between sex, gender, sexual practice and desire. Gender is performed through norms of intelligibility, which are historically and culturally constructed. Butler (1999: 34) posits: 'gender is not a noun, but neither is it a set of free-floating attributes, . . . the substantive effect of gender is performatively produced and compelled by the regulatory practices of gender coherence'. In this sense, Butler continues, 'there is no gender identity behind the expressions of gender; that identity is performatively constituted by the very 'expressions' that are said to be its results' (ibid.: 34).

It is crucial to emphasise the understanding of gender performativity, in which, the '"performative" dimension of construction is precisely the forced reiteration of norms'. Performativity is not to be understood as a theatrical representation, this reiteration and repetition of norms is not simply a performance of the subject, rather 'this repetition is what enables a subject and constitutes the temporal condition for the subject. . . . "Performance" is not a singular "act" or event, but a ritualised production, a ritual reiterated under and through constraint' (Butler, 1993: 95). Gender, in this sense, 'is the repeated stylisation of the body, a set of repeated acts within a highly rigid regulatory frame that congeal over time to produce the appearance of substance, of a natural sort of being' (Butler, 1999: 45).

Gender as a category is related to power relationships, to the social roles expected and spaces provided. This approach can also be seen in other categories, so, in the same way, understandings of race are treated in this book as performative, not a pre-given condition, rather a shifting signifier, seen within power relations as an effect of specific encounters.

Post-colonial studies provide important resources for this critical approach (Fanon, 1986; Gilroy, 2000; Balibar and Wallerstein, 2002; Hall, 2008; Bhabha, 2010; Hook, 2012). It is emphasised that race and culture are fluid constructions and vary according to different socio-political contexts. Nonetheless, it is on the historical fixity of some specific 'others' that discourses on race and culture are (re)produced having specific functions (Mountian and Lara, 2010). Thus, race refers here to regimes of difference, it produces specific others, socially politically located, produced and reproduced throughout history. So, in this sense, it is not on biological claims of race that this book engages with, but rather how discourses on race determines the subject's position (Gilroy, 2000). Balibar (1991) questions new forms of racism, more specifically on discourses on culture, whereby xenophobia is at stake:

> It's a racism whose dominant theme is not biological heredity but the insurmountability of cultural differences, a racism which, at first sight, does not postulate the superiority of certain groups or peoples in relation to others but 'only' the harmfulness of abolishing frontiers, the incompatibility of life-styles and traditions, in short, it is what P.A. Taguieff has rightly called *a differentialist racism*.

Here, it is important to consider the discursive replacement from 'race' to 'culture', and how 'culture' has been used in discourse. As Žižek (1998: 168) highlights, quoting Michaels (1992: 682–685), 'Our sense of culture is characteristically meant to displace race, but . . . culture has turned out to be a way of continuing rather than repudiating racial thought.'

These discourses place the subject in a specific position, that is, of the other. In the othering process, it is crucial to understand that 'minoritisation' of some specific others is done through encounters (Chantler, 2007); and that, importantly, this encounter is not symmetric, as Ahmed (2000: 11) points out, 'colonial encounters involve a necessarily unequal and asymmetric dialogue between once distant cultures that transforms each one'.

The notion of the other will be used in the analysis based on Foucault's elaboration on the gaze (Chapter 5), the social production of the other (Chapter 5), and on Lacanian psychoanalytic insights into the imaginary other, and the symbolic Other (Chapter 6).

This theoretical background emphasises an ethical approach of the need to acknowledge silenced or misrepresented groups, and as post-colonial studies, feminist research and queer studies made clear, it is crucial to challenge notions taken as natural categories (sex vs. gender, race vs. ethnicity/culture) by considering power within social structures, which are key epistemological standpoints for the reading of drugs, drug addiction and drug users proposed in this book.

3 Historical discourses of drugs

This chapter highlights key discourses in the history of drugs. Aiming to grasp elements of the social imaginary of drugs and drug users, I focus on key events in the history of drugs and highlight their social climate, particularly around gender, sexuality, race and class. From Foucault's philosophy, it is clear that the historical context is central to the understanding of meaning production.

Clearly, there is no straightforward history (of drugs). Traditional methodology of history searches for continuity, for repetitions of series and the effects it produces. Foucault (2002/1969: 11) argues for a deconstruction of such approach, where what is at stake is not a 'total' history, but rather, a 'general' history, where the aim is to:

> determine what form of relation may be legitimately described between these different series, what vertical system they are capable of forming, what interplay of correlation and dominance exists between them, what may be the effect of shifts, different temporalities, and various rehandlings, in what distinct totalities certain elements may figure simultaneously.

In this way, analysis of discontinuities, to the series of series, to disruptions, to what is not said, and identification of dominant positions, is paramount. In this sense, a critical reading considers power relations established in discourse and the effects of particular discourses. For example, taking up the history of medicine, what appears to be neutral, when closely examined, it is possible to see the emergence of a specific ethics that produces particular effects. Hence, what is called medicine is produced within a 'series of associations between events distributed along a number of different dimensions, with different histories, different conditions of possibility, different surfaces of emergence' (N. Rose, 1994: 50).

Foucault (2002/1969: 36) highlights how medicine in the nineteenth century was characterised by a style, a specific way of statements. Here, medicine inaugurated 'a corpus of knowledge that presupposed the same way of looking at things', to divide, to analyse and to describe. The clinical discourse concerns ethical choices, and a specific ethics of life, of regulations, models and descriptions. The clinical discourse thus gives an epistemological value – it becomes intelligible (Osborne, 1994). As such, understandings of drugs are crucial for this dynamic.

In this chapter, I focus on key aspects of the history of drugs, more specifically in relation to changes of societal, ideological and moral views regarding drugs. The objective of this chapter in highlighting these passages of the history of drugs is to provide the terrain for subsequent analysis of discourses on drugs, that is, practices and approaches to drug use, and contemporary imaginaries of the drug user and their intersections with gender, race and class.

Before we move on, I would like to emphasise some aspects on how to read this chapter as warranted by the epistemological and methodological frameworks put forward in Chapter 2. First, this chapter does not focus on specific details and full accounts of facts of the history of drugs, but rather it focuses on some key issues of the history in order to provide an epistemological perspective, attempting to identify some 'discursive unities', 'rules', 'categories', 'repetitions' in discourses, and the effects and moral grounds these produce. Second, the historical aspects emphasised are concerned with discourses of drugs as related to the changes of the imaginary of drugs and intersections with categories such as gender, class and race, through the contextualisation of the object-drug within broader political realms, religious moralities and medical discourses in Western countries.

When making gender relevant, I do not focus solely on women, rather the objective is to make gender, race and class visible within discourses about drugs and, at the same time, to highlight how these social structures operate within the drug arena. This is not a perspective on women and drugs *per se*, but rather it aims to deconstruct what is given at hand, challenging discourses on drugs and gender. As McDonald (1994: 1) points out, 'gender is about the various ways in which notions of "man" and "woman" are constructed'. This analysis takes into account the intersections between sexuality, race, class and age. Here, in the same way, race is not understood as a biological fixed category, but how understandings of race are constituted, that is, how discourses around race are constituted, considering racist and xenophobic discourses and the production of subjectivity.

This chapter identifies in events, statements and unities of discourse; it critically examines their emergence and position dominant discourses. The examples drawn upon will serve to juxtapose as well as oppose mainstream conceptions on drugs. The chapter outlines key aspects of modern liberal medicine (biomedicine). Although some examples from some Western countries are signalled, emphasis is given to policies designed in the US and UK because of their impact to the understanding of drugs worldwide, particularly the US role in the prohibition of (specific) drugs. This chapter will follow a chronological order.

Definitions of drugs and addiction

> The term 'drugs' is an extremely problematic one, connoting things such as abuse and addiction. For all its baggage, the word has one great virtue. It is short.
>
> (Courtwright, 2001: 2)

The first question to ask is: what are drugs? In fact, this question is posed throughout this book. There are numerous definitions and classifications of drugs from different traditions, such as the medical, juridical and religious. These approaches vary according to the social function of the drug, such as food, medicine, poison, for recreational use, social habits and religious rituals (Xiberras, 1989; McKenna, 1992; Goodman *et al.*, 1995; Escohotado, 1998; MacRae, 1998; South, 1999; Courtwright, 2001; Labate *et al.*, 2008). This chapter will focus on the medical and legal classifications of drugs, and on the importance of religious (moral) discourses in this field, as in contemporary Western societies these have become central to the understanding of drugs and drug users.

A commonly accepted medical definition of drugs concerns any chemical exogenous substance that provokes functional and/or structural alterations in any sector of the organic economy. From this first definition of drugs, two aspects can be highlighted. First, drugs are considered to be all the substances that cause alteration in the body, including legal and illegal drugs, regardless of the effects of the drug, and whether for medical or recreational purpose. Second, this descriptive definition does not account for the meanings and practices of drug taking, hence key classifications of drugs concern those used in law between licit and illicit drug use, or for the medical and psychiatric divisions that respond to the effects of drugs and their application in medicine. The World Health Organization (WHO) classifies drugs as:

> (i) A term of varied usage. In medicine, it refers to any substance with the potential to prevent or cure disease or enhance physical or mental welfare; in pharmacology it means any chemical agent that alters the biochemical or physiological processes of tissues or organisms. (ii) In the context of international drug control, 'drug' means any of the substances in Schedule I and II of the 1961 Convention, whether natural or synthetic. And psychotropic substance as: (i) any chemical agent affecting the mind or mental processes (i.e., any psychoactive drug). (ii) In the context of international drug control, 'psychotropic substance' means any substance, natural or synthetic, or any natural material in Schedule I, II, III or IV of the 1971 Convention'. Further WHO points out that the 'usage of the term 'illicit drug' should be avoided, as it is the manufacture, distribution, use etc. of a drug which is illicit, but not the substance itself.
>
> (United Nations Office for Drug Control and Drug Prevention, 2003)

This classification highlights the association between the medical and juridical realms, which is key to the understanding of the social imaginary of drugs and drug users. It inaugurates a new era of drugs: medical regulation and drug control. However, this classification still does not provide a clear definition, as too wide a range of substances are classified as drugs, not having a chemical unity. McMurran (1994) highlights this by arguing that although many substances (from aspirin to heroin) are called drugs, only some are understood as addictive. In fact, the concept of drugs is seen as a 'social artefact' (Gossop, 1982 in McMurran, 1994: 3). These ambiguous discursive positions of drugs have been pointed out by commentators, highlighting that, while there is a war on drugs, pharmacies advertise 'drugs' in neon signs (Lenson, 1995; South, 1999).

Analysing commonalities among drugs, Plant (1999) suggests that the ups and downs, highs and lows of drugs are ups and downs of tempo and speed. In this sense, drugs share the ability to change the speed of perception and the perception of speed. But we are still left with an open field for definition.

Another term commonly used for drugs is 'narcotics', seen in medical and law fields as well as in popular understandings and media. Originally, the word narcotic comes from the Greek *narkoun* meaning to sleep or sedate (Escohotado, 1998). Although the World Health Organization classifies narcotic drugs in medicine as a 'chemical agent that induces stupor, coma, or insensibility to pain (also called narcotic analgesic)' (United Nations Office for Drug Control and Drug

Prevention, 2003), in contemporary discourses, this term is applied for a wide range of drugs that, on the one hand, are not narcotics and, on the other hand, include too many different substances that have different effects among them (such as cocaine, marijuana, heroin), thus bringing more uncertainty to the definition.

For the legislative, drugs are referred to specific classifications of drugs – those concerning legal and illegal drugs, having a major impact for understandings of drugs. In this sense, Arnao (2002: 1) argues that the scientific word narcotic became a legal-bureaucratic term that defines these substances according to their legal status: 'The word "narcotics" had been purged of its scientific meaning and became, instead, a symbol of socially disapproved drugs'.

The classification of drugs between legal and illegal is said to be arbitrary in relation to the effects and functions of drugs (Loose, 2002a). Loose questions when a drug becomes medicine, and asks: does a drug become medicine by medical prescription?

As seen, definitions of drugs are not very specific, and the problem of defining drugs in history has been emphasised (Escohotado, 1998), in which for many decades there was an effort to design a classification of drugs. 'The international authority for public health declared that the problem is insoluble because of its extra-pharmacological spheres, thus proposing to classify drugs as legal and illegal' (ibid.: vol. 1, p. 21). The impossibility of establishing chemical or physiological criteria illustrates the problematic of the drug area, where the function of drugs concerns social values and moral domains.

Hence, discourses on drugs extrapolate the materiality of the substances themselves, including social and moral values related to the manipulability of drugs. In this way, the concept of addiction plays a central role for this discussion.

In relation to addiction, the same problem persists, leaving the understanding of addiction ambiguous and paradoxical. Commentators argue that drug addiction has become a matter of convention, and not of pharmacological specificities (Szasz, 1975; Bucher, 1992). When the focus is on addiction, what is at stake are not the substances themselves, but the behaviour towards chemical substances or things, therefore reflecting current social values: 'The substance is always the cultural values invested in it, and this applies whether the values be those of the police, the pharmacologist or the user' (McDonald, 1994: 19). Therefore, for the current discussion on discourses of drugs, it seems that drugs and their immediate counterpart, addiction, cannot be discursively separated. In Chapter 4, I explore in more detail definitions of addiction, and moral dichotomies implied within drug terminologies.

For the religious understandings of drugs, most Christian traditions consider drugs evil, impure substances that should be extinguished, when not used by the rituals themselves (Escohotado, 1998). In the case of religious rituals, these substances are understood as 'sacred substances': 'Christ's blood' for alcohol, or in other religious contexts as 'plants of power' (in the Brazilian religious use of ayahuasca in 'Santo Daime').

Hence, the definition of drugs appears fluid, and this gives space for various interpretations, having specific discursive effects. Thus, drugs themselves as mere things (entities) only have meaning when they are in order to; they have a function and a manipulability that confers their characteristics and, at the same time, refers to the subject who manipulates them in specific contexts. In the same vein, Vargas (2008), drawing on Deleuze and Guattari (1997), refers to drugs as socio-techno objects, which are those objects kept indeterminate until reported to those agencies that constitute them as such.

Heidegger (1997), referring to 'things', called them those entities in which there is an encounter that concerns 'equipment'. However, there is no such a thing as equipment isolated from its context:

> Equipment is essentially 'something in order to . . .' A totality of equipment is constituted by various ways of the 'in-order-to', such as serviceability, conduciveness, usability, manipulability.
>
> (p. 97)

> In the 'in-order-to' as a structure there lies an *assignment* or *reference* of something to something.
>
> (p. 97)

> Equipment – in accordance with its equipmentality – always *is in terms* of its belonging to other equipment: ink-stand, pen, ink, paper . . .
>
> (p. 97)

For example, a room is not four walls, but the encounter is the equipment for residing. 'The hammering itself uncovers the specific "manipulability" of the hammer. The kind of Being which equipment possesses – in which it manifests itself in its own right – we call "readiness-to-hand"' (ibid.: 98).

From these notions, it is possible to argue that, rather than having some inherent specific quality, *drugs consist of what are used as drugs and stipulated as such*. It is in the use of the substances that this particular entity is transformed into what is socially stipulated as a drug.

This notion is particularly important here. If the focus is on the use of drugs, drugs lose their original status. This means that the substantiality of drugs, the chemical composition, is not at stake here, but rather the meaning and signification towards substances, given according to the convention in particular social contexts.

Although there is no unity and clear definition of drugs and addiction, these medical definitions are central to the understanding of drugs and drug use in contemporary Western societies, and prohibition can be seen as the cornerstone of contemporary understandings of drugs. Further, for not having a clear definition, or having a malleable definition (see Chapter 4 discussion on *pharmakon*), drugs serve a range of purposes, specific practices and political functions.

Drugs and prohibition

The use of psychoactive plants throughout history and in practically all societies has attracted considerable attention (Douglas, 1987; Heath, 1987; McKenna, 1992; Escohotado, 1998). Escohotado argues that all communities have used psychoactive substances, with the exception of communities based in the Arctic zones, where the climate does not provide the conditions for the existence of vegetation. The use of psychoactive substances constitutes, therefore, a plural phenomenon. These uses vary according to their time, places and purposes.

Thus, this consumption is intrinsically related to social and cultural values and habits within specific historical periods (Berridge and Edwards, 1987; Xiberras, 1989; Goodman *et al.*, 1995; Escohotado, 1998; Benitez, 2000). For example, an ethnographic approach to alcohol allows us to witness a wide range of beliefs and behaviours in relation to alcohol, hence bringing us to conclude that 'the outcomes of its use are mediated by cultural factors rather than chemical, biological, or other pharmaco-physiological factors' (Heath, 1987: 19). In the same way, understandings of alcohol as a problem and disease is socially produced, specific to cultural and historical contexts, and as such, ideas of behaviours resulting from alcohol, particularly violent behaviour (usually male), are also culturally located; whereas this behaviour is learnt, and it is not universal (McDonald, 1994).

Practically all societies have developed knowledge about psychoactive substances for therapeutic purposes, religious-ritualistic contexts and habitual use. Some examples, among many, include the Sumerian use of opium in 5000 BC (Szasz, 1975), which is the first drug that was written about (Escohotado, 1998: vol. 1); the description of a brewery in an Egyptian papyrus in 3500 BC; the use of tea in China around 3000 BC (Szasz, 1975); the medicinal plants in ancient Greece (Escohotado, 1998: vol. 1); and the use of psychoactive substances by the pre-Colombian indigenous populations (McKenna, 1992). From this, it is possible to argue that each drug has its own characteristics and distinct history. But how do these relate to the contemporary scene?

While it may not be possible to examine this within a causal frame, attempting to look at the transformation of meaning (discourse) in history, it is possible to find some 'categories' and some understandings that approximate these different cultures. One key aspect that can be highlighted is the intervention of law as a distinguishing mark between the classic and contemporary forms of intoxication. Xiberras (1989) suggests that the classic practice of drug use did not cause rejection from the societies where they were developed, but rather they were part of traditions and social practices, for example alcohol in the Western world and cannabis in the Oriental world. Modern addiction refers to the practices of the last two centuries, practices that have the disapproval of authorities and a negative reaction from the judicial power. Hence, the intervention of law is of major importance to the understanding of contemporary drug use, representing an ideological shift.

Here, it is important to point out that *the intervention of law draws the distinction between legal and illegal drug use, and discursively this has come to imply the difference between medical and non-medical drugs*, apart from some drugs that are used in everyday life that are not discursively referred to as drugs, such as coffee and tea.

The term 'drug' therefore becomes 'a password automatically implying a prohibition' (Ruggiero, 1999: 123). In this sense, it is relevant to point out an example suggested by Young (1971), in which a morphine injection is a legal and fortunate act when applied to the terminally ill, but it is an act involving the consequences of law when used by a street 'junkie'.

While the intervention of law is explored throughout this book in various ways, it is possible to point out here some consequences of the criminalisation of drugs, such as the invisibility of illegal drug use making it difficult to gather statistics, information on the economy, reliable information on production and consumption (Hugh-Jones, 1995), as well as in all the problematic aspects of the context involving the market of drugs as crime – consuming, producing and selling.

What does this law represent and what are the foundations for these laws? What do these specific discourses evoke? How do law and medicine operate within discourses of health? And, furthermore, how has addiction come to be seen as a problem? Taking a historical perspective brings some insights into the foundations of these discursive practices.

Escohotado (1998: vol. 2) proposes five main arguments for the context of prohibition and drug control: the traditional religious element (impurity); social tensions in relation to the working class and industrialisation (drugs symbolising the deviation of certain groups – Chinese, Mexican, black people); the establishment of the medical profession (like the ecclesiastics of other times); the state assuming functions that before were performed by civil society (welfare state); and the Chinese-English conflict (highlighting stereotypes and colonial relations). I also include here gender as another key aspect (e.g. fear of interracial marriages). Thus, it is essential to take into account macro-social levels, from politics to moral heritage around this issue. For this purpose, key historical events will now be discussed to help visualise the social climate for this prohibition. I start by situating opium in England in the nineteenth century, in which ideas such as addiction as a disease were developed, and also how these ideas collaborated for the establishment of the medical profession.

I focus on the UK and US drug policies because of their major impact on drug policies worldwide, particularly on the North American role in international drug control and prohibition. Although the history of drugs in the US and UK differ, they converge in certain aspects, such as the moral influence for the imaginary of drugs, and the predominant medical approach and control on drugs, which have become the most influential perspectives in drug policies in Western countries. Further, the understanding of women as potential victims of drug use, the connection between drugs and ethnic minorities, and issues on social class are also found in both settings.

History of drugs: addiction as disease and religious movements

During the nineteenth and twentieth centuries, the concept of addiction shifted from habit to disease and social problem. The notion of addiction as a disease constitutes the major model for contemporary medical research and practice, for the legal classification of drugs and popular discourses on drugs. A key element that is explored in this section concerns the moral values that underline this conception. This aspect appears in both US and UK history, influenced by the Protestant and Temperance movements.

I begin by highlighting some aspects in the history of opium in the UK because it illustrates well this change of climate concerning drugs during this period (nineteenth and twentieth centuries), which continue to prevail today.

A first aspect to notice is how discourses on health were closely associated with morality. In the eighteenth and nineteenth centuries, alcohol came to be perceived as a problem in the US and the UK. McDonald (1994) argues that, through its availability and increasing consumption, together with the new social relations accompanying industrialisation, alcohol turned into a serious threat to the economic and moral order. Abstinence was then equivalent to respect, self-control, hard work and thriftiness; all qualities indicative of religious commitment and economic prosperity.

The notion of health implied abstinence from alcohol, so that a healthy person was a symbol of a good and ruled life; self-control represented good character, of being moral and pure. In this way, the term 'health', seen as cultural-specific, was embedded with these moral values. These discourses on health and inebriety contributed to the later formulation of addiction as a disease.

Developed in the UK and US, this approach was highly influenced by positivism, explaining behaviour on the basis of methods of natural science. The underlying idea of addiction being a disease of the will, then a disease, led both countries to an understanding of addiction close to criminality, underground sub-cultures and an emphasis on control and prohibition of drugs (Zieger, 2008).

Religious movements had an important impact in areas considered morally deviant, such as 'homosexualism' (as it was termed) and inebriety, and as such, these movements were a major influence for the conception of addiction. The evils of alcohol were given confirmation over the same period by the idea that what had previously been known as '"habitual drunkenness" was in fact a disease' (McDonald, 1994: 2). Inebriety was a term used for a number of drugs, gaining prominence in the late nineteenth century given by former Temperance activists and physicians (Zieger, 2008), and, in the mid-twentieth century, it fell out of use, being later replaced by alcoholism, addiction or dependency (White, 2004).

Initially in the US, the notion of 'addiction' was related to the Protestant notion of self-control, whereby drug addicts were seen as having a 'disease of the will', not controlling themselves and experiencing 'craving' for alcohol. This same notion dominated later understandings of drugs. In Britain, for the Temperance movement – influential during the nineteenth and twentieth centuries – there was a belief in the sin and degradation of alcohol consumers (Gusfield, 1997).

The Temperance movement proposed moderation for the good of society, focusing on problems of alcohol. The American Temperance

Society was formed in 1826, and it first arrived in England in Liverpool, where the Liverpool Temperance Society was founded in 1830. In Scotland, the Moderation Society was founded in 1828 (Harrison, 1971).

The Temperance movement in Britain was first associated with abstainers from spirits. Teetotal societies were increasing, and by the 1830s, some teetotallers adopted the 'long pledge', banning the offer and consumption of intoxicants. The British and Foreign Temperance Society was a London-based reforming society following the traditional evangelical model. Here, Quakers and women were prominent.

During the nineteenth century, Temperance ideas focused on alcohol, singling it out as a particularly dangerous substance. 'The moral, religious, political and legal spotlights turned alcohol in such a way that it appeared, of itself, capable of producing social effects of all kinds' (McDonald, 1994: 3). Alcohol was viewed as an evil substance *per se*, the source of addiction, promoting here the idea of individual vulnerability, and drunkenness was considered a sin.

For opium, a new climate was about to emerge. In the nineteenth century, opium was not seen as a disease nor as deviant in the UK; rather, the use of opium for medical or semi-medical purposes was generally accepted (Berridge, 1989). In 1868, with the Pharmacy Act, opium use started to be controlled, although restrictions were still quite minimal and many formulas using opium were still available (Berridge and Edwards, 1987). Consumed by all levels of society, opium was regarded as a domestic medicine for all sorts of minor complaints, including excessive drinking. Although historically more attention has been given to the recreational use of opium, the main use was self-medication and, in general, opium use was not viewed as a 'problem'. As Dally (1996: 203) points out, 'addicts, formerly objects of mild disapproval, rather like drunks or smokers today, were gradually turned into criminals and outcasts'.

The use of opium by romantic poets (an upper class use of drugs), illustrates this change of opinion and media exaggeration. In the early nineteenth century, the use of opium by writers (e.g. De Quincey, Samuel Taylor Coleridge) attracted much attention, even though there was quite extensive popular use. The public response to *Confessions of an English Opium Eater* by De Quincey (1821) in *The London Magazine* (1821) was initially excitement and, although for some groups it was a moral issue, in general the reaction was of interest and not panic (Berridge and Edwards, 1987).

The habit of opium use of these writers illustrates the intertwining of the 'social' and 'medical' use of opium. Opium was used for social consumption and self-medication by the middle and working classes (e.g. in the fens of East England), and the users were not regarded as ill or addicted (McDonald, 1994).

> Many managed their dependence without the physical and mental deterioration, the social incapacity, or the early death which is the stereotype of contemporary narcotic addiction. Addiction, in fact, was not the point at issue for those users of the drug and their contemporaries.
>
> (Berridge and Edwards, 1987: 61)

However, in the late 1830s, concerns about opium use started to increase, and such usage was no longer tolerated. A climate of opinion was formed in which opium use was no longer an everyday part of life for all sections of society, and doctors became particularly involved in the control of the use of opium.

> From being one among many prescribers of the drug, with nothing approaching unitary control, they began to re-define opium use as solely a medical imprint, it became a disease, a habit warranting medical intervention. Doctors became the custodian of a problem which they had helped define.
>
> (ibid.: 76)

Two aspects regarding the medical discourse merit emphasis here: the creation of addiction as a disease, which became the main contemporary discourse surrounding drugs (particularly the criminalised ones); and the association between opium control and the rise of the medical profession and monopoly.

Although mortality was not high in relation to the frequency of use, it became an important argument for health campaigns. Poisoning from opium was mainly the result of extensive adulteration of the drug (as well as food and beer) and the different kinds of opium available. At the end of the century, adulteration of opium was uncommon, however the risk of adulteration and overdosing also contributed to the new view of opium (Berridge and Edwards, 1987). The focus on opium death rates was therefore, in a sense, a form of professional self-definition and self-validity for the status of doctors' expertise.

Regarding the alliance between the state and the medical profession, this move to end or reduce opium poisoning was important for the medical professional movement of the 1850s and 1860s, where the state gave support to the medical area, and statistics were used as public health propaganda. This cooperation and a drug-centred approach are at the kern of contemporary drug policies. Berridge and Edwards (1987: 78) point out:

> Concentration on simple statistical results without an awareness of social context or economic reality produced a situation which justified the restriction of open sale of the drug. Opium, as elsewhere, was the scapegoat for broader defects in the society of the time.

This alliance is of major importance to critical approaches to health, and in this case, drug policies. Two key features are highlighted here: the politics of drugs, i.e. how discourses of drugs are used strategically for political purposes (e.g. political power in Chapter 5), and how medicine came to prescribe an ethics of living, as further elaborated in Chapter 4.

At this point, it is possible to identify three major discursive foundations surrounding drug use and their relations, the religious influence (evangelical and temperance movements), growing status of the medical profession (expansion of psychiatry), and state regulations.

While medicine as an organised institution had its basis in the nineteenth century, it was not until the twentieth century that the organisational structure of the profession was established as seen nowadays. It was in the 1830s that the medical profession started to become more clearly defined, and the 'birth' of psychiatry had its origins during this period, which was separated from medicine. The practitioners were known as 'alienists' who worked in asylums. Lunbeck (1994) points out that medicine was a combination of moral and religious thoughts, therefore carrying punitive practices. Psychiatry started occupying an important position in relation to identifying and classifying pathologies, where diagnosis was an essential element of its practice. Only few would challenge the diagnosis and, in fact, they would on the contrary expect psychiatrists to determine if the person was ill, insane or in need of care.

Hence, medicine, and more precisely medical discourse, is not conferred solely within the hospitals, but rather medical discourses are seen in everyday life, in the pathologisation and psychologisation of subjects, playing therefore a formative role in subjectivity. N. Rose (1994) argues that medicine is constitutively social, not only that it has to be understood in a social context, but it also constitutes the way in which society has been thought about. Rose highlights that society, as it is historically invented, is immediately accorded an organic form and thought of in medical terms:

> As a *social body* it is liable to sickness: that is to say, it is problematised in the vocabulary of medicine. As a social body it needs to be restored to health: that is to say, its government is conceptualised in medical terms.
>
> (ibid.: 54)

Medicine, therefore, 'has played a formative role in the *invention of the social*' (ibid.: 55). Here, we see the basis of a specifics ethics of life and social intervention within these terms.

The analysis of poisoning and treatment of opium use was also the basis for the disease theory of addiction. Treatment involved physical methods too. For example, in the 1840s, the Galvanic method (electric shock) was used to treat opium poisoning. This model fell out of use at the end of the century (Berridge and Edwards, 1987).

With the use of the hypodermic, the medical profession became concerned with the repeated use of morphine when injected. In 1877, Dr Levinstein (in Berlin) defined 'morphinism' as a disease similar to dipsomania, but not a mental disease. Also in this period, 'alcoholism' (a relatively new term) became seen as a disease (ibid.). Alcoholism is a term coined by a Swedish physician Magnus Huss in 1849 for chronic intoxication (White, 2004). This term only took currency in the mid-twentieth century, despite debates on the precision of the term. For example, in 1941, Jellinek proposed fourteen types of alcohol problematic intake (ibid.).

It was during this period that the medicalisation of deviant behaviour was further developed and the case of morphinism was important here. Although there was little evidence of large numbers of morphine addicts and no sub-culture of morphine use, during the 1880s case histories of morphine addicts started to replace studies of morphine use in the medical journals, and ideas such as women being susceptible to morphinism, together with the idea of female weakness, started to emerge.

Opium use for women was indicated for female complaints such as, dysmenorrhoea or menstrual pain, in childbirth, as a palliative for a number of complaints, and for 'nervous disorder', a notion that already carries a gender bias. 'Hysterical women' were medicated with hypodermic morphine, and the problem of consequent self-administration and abuse was originated by this practice. Notwithstanding this, there were more male than female consumers (Berridge and Edwards, 1987). Morphine was seen as a prescription mostly for women, for 'bourgeois femininity' (Keire, 1998: 809), in the US most of medical addicts were women and there was a spread idea that addiction was feminine.

By 1900, medicine was more technologically developed (with immunisation, bacterial research), organised and recognised. Acker (1996: 115) describes three aims of the American Medical Association: 'to transform therapeutics along modern and scientific lines, to increase medical control over drugs and to prevent the practices of careless or mercenary physicians', including tackling self-medication. Another redefinition was seen in relation to the use of psychotropic drugs, from one drug for different illnesses, they promoted the idea of specific drugs for specific illnesses (Moncrieff, 2008). Opium, in this sense, was a central area of concern.

Following this chronology, by the end of the nineteenth century, cannabis and cocaine came to be seen as dangerous narcotics – neither of these substances are in fact narcotic drugs in the proper sense of the word. In England during this period, the non-medical use of cocaine was not common, whereby cannabis and opium smoking were favoured. This was different from the US and Europe, where recreational use of cocaine was higher than in the UK in the 1890s. Progressively, opium use lost its place in popular culture and was not central in medical practice any longer. Self-medication decreased, although giving opium (*laudanum*) in the baby's bottle among the working class was still a popular practice in the Britain (Berridge and Edwards, 1987).

However, opiate addiction came to be seen as a social threat: the addict gradually was turned into a personality type with deficits in need of adjustment, and addiction came to be equated with loss of all moral senses (ibid.). These views of opium use could also be seen in the US in the same period, where users were portrayed as weak, pitiful people who became attached to a habit (Acker, 1996). The disease theory, therefore, is a key aspect for contemporary discourses of drugs. It reproduces and promotes a specific discourse, as Berridge and Edwards (1987: 229) point out:

> The disease view of addiction with its implicit notions of constitutional or hereditary predisposition established an individualistic, privatising ideology, nominally value-free. Medical concepts reinforced and reflected existing social structures. A distinct area of ideological terrain had been won.

In the US, by the early twentieth century, medicine conceived of addiction as a bio-psychological condition. For the physiological model, it was the substance that would induce addiction, and the psychological model centred on the psychology of the user and believed that pre-existing psychological elements (inherent neurosis, congenital manic depression) would make people susceptible to drug addiction. 'The contemporary support for eugenics, as well as the concern with psychopathic criminality among scholars and criminal justice professionals provided a very conducive atmosphere to these theories' (Ghatak, 2010: 48). In both cases, the social aspects and understanding of drugs within their social context were not taken into account.

Hence, the nineteenth century was fundamental to the current understandings of drugs, and crucially of health, and for the establishment of the medical profession, the alliance with the state and the moral influence of religious groups. As N. Rose (1994) points out, the nineteenth century established various apparatuses related to health, and these do not concern only medical practice, but rather they are related to the public space, for fighting diseases. The domestic sphere was then subject to scrutiny and regulation on the basis of medical terms; alliances and dependencies between mothers and doctors played an important role here. During the twentieth century, these medical and health regulations entered schools and working places, transforming them into 'inspection machines' and institutions 'gridded by norms of health' (ibid.: 63). Hence, this regime provided a new rationality in which security has to be maximised by calculating the risks.

Drugs as menace: a nation under threat

The medical view and criminalisation of some drugs have had a fundamental impact on the social imaginary of drugs and drug users and considering the intersections between gender, 'race' and class. In the twentieth century, drugs came to be seen as the great menace of society (in both the UK and US), and addiction had a particular role within this context.

Before prohibition, discourses on drug users had a different configuration: 'although they were seen as fiends, drug addicts were not greatly feared' (Kohn, 1992: 18). They were endangering themselves, and not society; and they were not yet criminals. Since there were no laws against possession, drugs could be bought in the pharmacy without prescription. Nevertheless, after the First World War, this image was about to change.

When society was in crisis, the construction of drugs as a social menace started to appear. This fear of drugs was based on certain features and contexts, such as drugs being seen as a cult activity taken at clandestine locations, the belief that young women were the most at risk of the 'drug habit' and association with sexual immorality. From this came the view that the worst evil of drugs was that they facilitated the seduction of young women by 'men of colour' (Kohn, 1992).

As Zieger (2008: 9) highlights, the British and North American 'cultural histories of addiction both form around a mobile concept of colonial seduction leading inexorably to a debilitating imperial dependency and compulsion', drawing on ideas of addiction close to slavery, which forms the antithesis of the merging free and modern Enlightenment thinking. This contextualised North American notion of freedom began its imperial expansion, to the point that the history of addiction came to be equated to the history of drug control (ibid.).

Fear of mixing race was also prevalent in the US, where drug policies were planned to protect white women, and so enhancing the dangerousness accorded to black men. This was also due to the late idea that white women were less resistant both to the pleasure and the deteriorations generated by drugs, 'a delicate female having light blue eyes and flaxen hair, possesses, according to my observation the maximum susceptibility' (H. Kane, physician in Campbell, 2000: 68). In this context, the use of drugs by a white person was seen as an 'individual aberration', whereas for 'people of colour', as well as for the working class, it was regarded as more 'natural'.

During the First World War and in the post-war period, xenophobia and nationalism were prevalent, and drugs played an important role within this scenario: 'There were other foes to be confronted besides the German enemy – first, alcohol, and then cocaine. Spies and drunken women were obsessions of the newspapers and the efficiency of the war effort a concern for Government' (South, 1994: 1).

Fear and crisis in British society grounded a xenophobic approach to drug use, and this perspective is examined in several cases connecting together 'vice, race, corruption and drugs' (ibid.: 2). It is important to note that after the First World War, the xenophobic climate was still prevalent (against the Germans and later against the Jews, Russians, Swiss and Chinese). Within this context, alcohol came to be seen as a problem, and governmental initiatives were taken in order to discipline the population, concerned with industrial production and public order. By the influence of the Temperance movement, alcohol was selected as a scapegoat: '"We are fighting Germans, Austrians and Drink, and so far as I can see, the greatest of these deadly foes is Drink", Lloyd George declared in 1915' (Kohn, 1992: 28).

The most familiar example of this regime is the closure of pubs in the afternoon, remaining in the English statutes until 1988. In 1915, the Home Secretary, with temporary provision Acts, imposed a midnight curfew at weekends for clubs, and restaurants and pubs could serve food only until 9.30 p.m. This created the conditions for the emergence of illegal nightclubs, as with the curfew, clubs became underground, and by 1915 they were widespread (150 illegal nightclubs in Soho alone). Alcohol was then highly regulated and nightlife became private or illegal, which also provided the conditions for the drug scene (Kohn, 1992).

It was also during this period that the US prohibited the recreational consumption of alcohol. Prohibition gave rise to the increase of the illegal market of alcohol, and a known outcome was the danger of death from poisonous illicit alcohol. Alcohol could be produced for scientific, industrial, medicinal and sacred purposes, and some doctors profited from prescribing whiskey (Royal College of Psychiatrists, 2000). Most North Americans were drinking less during prohibition, although alcohol was seen as abused by Irish immigrants (Rodrigues, 2003). Prohibition was the culmination of a long and well-organised political movement. Particularly campaigning for prohibition were Protestants (who were teetotal), industrialists (concerned with injuries and absenteeism at work) and the women's movement. Still, many were against such prohibition, particularly those from the cities (Tracy and Acker, 2004). Alcoholics Anonymous was founded in the 1930s.

It is worth emphasising the social context of alcohol consumption and its relationship to gender, class and race. Alcohol prohibition was most flout in the industrialised cities, where immigrants, including Italian and Irish Catholics, used saloons as the centre of trade union activities. In relation to gender, alcohol was not greatly consumed by women before prohibition, however during the 1920s women started to participate in male-only environments, forming a group of drinkers with habits different than the macho heavy drinking culture (Royal College of Psychiatrists, 2000).

During this period, in Britain, women too started occupying public positions and being seen in public in a rather different way. For example, in London, actresses, singers and dancers enjoyed a freedom unthinkable at that time, while young women were restrictedly controlled in dormitories and asking for permission to visit the theatre, identifying their companions. This public presence was highly sexualised 'a "public woman" was a prostitute' (Kohn, 1992: 52).

During the First World War, this image started to change, as the boundaries between public women and women in public blurred. It was in this period that women started to dine out without the company of men, and to smoke in public. However, the emergence of this new image provoked social reactions, as Kohn (1992: 53) points out, 'smoking is a sensual self-gratifying pleasure. Born to the assumption that women exist for others, male reactionaries (in the strict sense of the term) were unable to stomach the idea of women pleasing themselves'. The limited space for self-indulgence, and particularly body pleasures for women, is further explored in Chapter 6.

In relation to the social imaginary of 'public women vs. women in public' (Kohn, 1992), it is relevant to point out the negative images addressed to actresses at that time. Partly, this idea arises from the connection between public appearance and prostitution. Being in public for women was associated with being a public woman, thereby women's presence in the new night life was condemned. South (1994) highlights that negative social reactions towards women who use drugs reflect the dichotomous discourses on women, either respectable or those who deserved to be morally condemned.

During the First World War, it was not only alcohol, but also other drugs, such as cocaine, came to be seen as scapegoats. Stories spread out of prostitutes using drugs to knock out their victims, or young women portrayed as victims of men because of drugs and later becoming prostitutes. Cocaine, which before had a mixed reputation, became a threat. During the war, it was feared that soldiers were taking cocaine (McDonald, 1994), and stories of prostitutes giving cocaine to soldiers to steal from them (South, 1994), were also prevalent. In fact, this is another important aspect in the politics of drugs – the threat to soldiers and the importance of the media in this context:

> *The Times* ran an article headlined 'the cocaine habit – soldier's temptation, which deemed the drug 'more deadly than bullets'. It asserted that the habit had reached India a few years previously, and was calculated to kill natives there within three months. Uncharacteristic for its time, in omitting any reference to women or sex, the piece instead gave cocaine an aura of violence: 'most cocainomaniacs carry revolvers to protect themselves from imaginary enemies'. It carried a patriotic flourish, claiming that the drug was mostly smuggled on Austrian steamers.
>
> (Kohn, 1992: 34)

In the US, similarly, by the beginning of the twentieth century, 'cocaine was said to destroy the moral senses, turning women into prostitutes, boys into thieves and men into hardened killers' (Courtwright, 1995: 10), and stories started to appear also targeting black people, linking crime (also of sexual nature) with cocaine use.

Keire (1998) highlights the use of opiates by prostitutes for 'female troubles' (medical use) and the moral discourses on this use, whereby it was believed that women could not be sexually aggressive, so they would use drugs to cope with this counter-nature. Condemnation on the pimp's drug use was also present. Furthermore, Keire highlights the Fairies' use of cocaine, and associations of this use with homosexuality became widespread at the beginning of the twentieth century.

These stories are situated in a context in which patriotism and nationalism were associated with virility and paternalism towards women. These ideas emerged with the new social changes, such as the changes in women's status, a period of transition. Paternalism and xenophobia could also be seen in the fear of mixing race and ideas around women's 'atavistic passions' induced by alcohol and drugs. In this way, these aspects of the post-war context were seen as jeopardising the male order, and a xenophobic and racist approach to drugs emerged as one of the outcomes.

As such, another group targeted during this period was the immigrant community. In the UK and US, there was fear of relationships between white women, Chinese men and the use of opium. This was referred to by the *Empire News* as the 'moral yellow peril' (Kohn, 1992). These discourses concern the fear of intermix of 'races', and the seduction of white women into gambling and drugs.

Kohn (1992) argues that the British did not fear so much gambling and opium, but rather the seduction of white women, so that the problem of vice was in relation to the attraction of women. Comparisons between Chinese gambling and opium were at stake, and gambling (*pai-ke-p'iao*) was regarded as worse than opium, although most of the demand for this cheap and illegal game came from white East Enders. In fact, the dangers claimed in gambling were the same as for drug use – that it was compulsive, led its users into poverty and to other vices, and women were the primary victims:

> The Chinese, it was said, allowed young women to win in order to snare them – in the same way that drug dealers are perennially alleged to hook new customers with free samples. Soon they were dragged into utter degradation.
>
> (ibid.: 61)

The opium ban gave the authorities a pretext to invade Chinese domestic privacy, and to stage exemplary deportations, intimidating the entire community. The Chinese and the Jamaicans played the role of the villain within drug narratives during this period (Kohn, 1992).

In the same vein, in the US, the association of Chinese immigrants was long established, seen in reports of the British Opium Wars of the 1840s, and the sensationalist media on the 'opium dens'. At the end of the nineteenth century and beginning of the twentieth, there was a growth in 'scientific stories' explaining the habit of drug use through the notion of addiction. However, most of the new visible 'addicts' were not Chinese or opium smokers (Hickman, 2000). Yet, argues Hickman (2000: 71), 'fear of the Chinese and the Black shaped America drug policy. This world of Oriental otherness thus threatened the stability of the bourgeois subject – while also defining it'. In this context, the Chinese were seen as spreading opium to an unwary nation.

We can identify three prevailing discursive registers of drug discourses within this context: the 'primitivising', the 'orientalising' and the 'sexualising':

> Early-twentieth-century drug discourse lined the age of dope to the practices of the 'oriental' through the figure of the 'white slaver'. The primitivised subcultural styles and sites of jazz clubs and dance halls, and the domestic and leisure activities of the working classes, recent immigrants, and African-American communities were also associated with the drug threat. The primitivising rhetoric applied to the lower and working classes; the orientalising register applied to the self-indulgence of the upper and middle classes – native-born women supplied by unscrupulous physicians, traffickers in women, and 'oriental drug smugglers'.
>
> (Campbell, 2000: 61)

The upper class use of drugs is seen in both the UK and US, as well as in many Western countries. These three discursive structures and its intersections – the primitivising (working class, immigrant), the orientalising (upper class use) and the sexualising (gender and sexuality) will be further developed next.

The establishment of drug control: race, class, gender and sexuality

Taking into account the changes in the image of drugs, now seen as the 'enemy', and intersections with gender (women), race (Chinese and black people) and class (working class), I concentrate on discourses on fear of addiction and drug use in relation to ethnic minorities generated during the nineteenth and twentieth centuries. Focusing on some key events in the North American history of drugs, I highlight the beginning of drug control and prohibition.

As pointed out earlier, since the nineteenth and twentieth centuries, addicts were identified with foreign groups and internal minorities against the background of an increasingly salient national identity. These groups were already feared, and the object of elaborated and massive (social and legal) constraints. The two main oppressed groups that were associated with the use of drugs were the Chinese (in relation to opium), and black people (in relation to cocaine). It is important to consider how race intersects with class here. As Zieger (2008: 242) highlights, the invention of the addict, draws on dichotomised discursive positions of the 'master and slave, consumer and producer, men and women, straight and queer, white and race, citizen and pathological criminal'.

By 1909, opium was banned in the US, and this ban was symbolically associated with Chinese consumption. Chinese people were persecuted and almost banned from immigrating to the US. In this context, Musto (1999) argues that the prohibition of smoking opium was also utilised as a symbolic mark that the US was fighting against the evils of addiction. Dally (1996) points out that the phrase 'drug abuse', meaning 'illegal drug use', was at first utilised in America as a disapproval of the Southern blacks' use of cocaine, and later this was extended to Chinese opium smoking (Zinberg, 1984):

> In an article in the *New York Medical Journal*, Dr. Perry Lichtenstein, a physician at the New York City Prison stated that drug habits vary according to racial identity (Lichtenstein, 1914: 965). Commenting on the increase in the use of cocaine in the urban vice districts, the chairman of the Committee on Acquirement of the Drug Habit of the American Pharmaceutical Association, Hynson (1902) asserted that prostitutes, African-Americans and Chinese immigrants are the most likely drug users.
>
> (Ghatak, 2010: 43)

It was during this period that a specific social imaginary of addicts was constructed, and fear of addiction was disseminated. Drugs were perceived as leading to slavery, a state of 'social death', and addiction was seen as a kind of bondage 'modelled on slavery that affected whites' (Campbell, 2000: 72). Indeed, this fear provided the scope for punitive methods against addicts and suppliers:

> For at least seventy years purveyors of these drugs for non-medical uses have been branded 'worse than murderers', in that destroying

> the personality is worse than simply killing the body. What is most human is what is destroyed in the drug habitués, the opponents of narcotics argued.
>
> (Musto, 1999: 5)

Fear plays a crucial role in the debates on drugs, as identified so far – fear of addiction, fear of alcohol, of opium, of morphine, of cocaine and now cannabis. In the 1920s, fear of cannabis was beginning to emerge, although the use was still minimal throughout the US. Notwithstanding this, it still concerned the federal government, and another ethnic group became associated – the Mexicans. Mexican areas where marijuana was used for entertainment were feared, this group came to be associated with crime and deviant behaviour, and the cause of marijuana use was often attributed to them. In 1919, there were reports stating that Mexican prisoners were violent because of the use of the drug and, in the mid-1920s, they were attributing hideous crimes to marijuana and its Mexican purveyors (Musto, 1999).

Until 1915, there was a more tolerant attitude in relation to addict maintenance (mainly by physicians), however during 1919 and 1920 drugs came to be seen as dangerous and foolish: 'advocacy of maintenance was repressed as sternly as socialism' (ibid.: 133). However, juridical change was not the majority of the people's opinion, but of an intolerant minority (Musto, 1999). These changes have to be seen in their social-political context. As Goldberg (1999) (drawing on Durkheim's theory of 'anomie') argues, this process is linked to the rapid changes of the twentieth century, in which norms and rules became obsolete, leading to confusion and fear. Drugs, in this context, became a symbol of what is unknown and frightening.

This social imaginary of drugs and drug users disseminated in the US, gave scope for their political pressure on to the main policies adopted worldwide. In 1909, there was the Shanghai conference, with the presence of countries such as China, the US, England, Germany, Holland, France and Portugal. This meeting resulted in the acceptance of the US proposal, although European states were not in complete agreement regarding the restriction of opium sale only for medical reasons. Rodrigues (2003) highlights the importance of this meeting because it inaugurated diplomatic meetings for the control of drugs.

In 1912 in Haia, another conference promoted by the US resulted in further restrictions of opium and cocaine sale and production, establishing a prohibitionist attitude in international scale, reinforcing the medical use and disapproving the recreational use of drugs. From Haia, the US implemented the Harrison Act (1914), prohibiting any use of psychoactive drugs if not for medical reasons. After this, there were two major meetings, in 1925 and 1941 in Genebra, and again the US defended prohibitionism and put pressure on other countries to create their own repressive departments against psychoactive substances (ibid.).

In this context, the Harrison Act worked to protect the 'nation' against addiction, which was seen as a 'threat to the national war effort' (Musto, 1999: 133). Drug campaigns were characteristically medico-penal, dispositive of regulation. This alarm, raised against the 'enemy' during the First World War, can also be seen in the English scene.

Although there was local regulation in some places, the Harrison Act was the first federal act for drug control. It was not a prohibition of drugs, but it intended to regulate the opium market, restricting the use for medical research and medical control. The state could also tax these imported substances for legitimate use, dealers and practitioners had to register, and their records were controlled (Ghatak, 2010). This legislation gave rise to the illegal drug market (McDonald, 1994).

From the Harrison Act, the Narcotics Division in the Internal Revenue Service of the Treasury Department was established, and a number of court decisions were amended reviewing medical misuse of drugs. This gave expansion and jurisprudence to the Narcotics Division. For example, in some cases against the Harrison Act, such as Doremus (1919), the Supreme Court decided on prosecution of unauthorised transactions. In Webb's case (1919), sale of opiates for people without prescription was against the law, as well as prescription for other reasons if not treatment. For Jin Fue Moy (1920), it was decided that prescription should follow strict guidelines, and other usages constituted a crime. For Behrman (1922), 'the Supreme Court opined that while doctors indeed can prescribe opiates, when the prescribed quantity exceeds a certain reasonable amount it might construe a ground for suspicion' (Ghatak, 2010: 45). From the Berhman case, a number of high-profile decisions were taken, such as raids into medical clinics.

In 1922, the Narcotic Drug Import and Export Act (Jones-Miller Act) determined penalties of 10 years imprisonment for anyone who dealt with unauthorised substances. In 1924, it prohibited the import and manufacture of heroin, because it was believed there was no scientific use, but solely recreational (ibid.).

While the moral discourse on drugs during the nineteenth century was influenced by the religious movement, in the twentieth century, medical discourse and state regulations came to replace these discourses. By the 1920s, a specific social imaginary of drugs was established, as possible of transforming people, destroying their soul, and turning them into slaves and a menace to society that could be spread across nation. Drugs should then be suppressed by law enforcement and should be imposed nationally and internationally. This view settled the terrain for the control of drugs in other countries. Although there were disagreements in international grounds, the US positioned that drugs should be strictly controlled. In 1931, the Narcotics Convention of Geneva approved the main American demands on the production and trade of opium:

> The US ratified the resultant treaty in April 1932 that came into effect in July 10, 1933 with forty signatory nations. The Geneva Convention required the signatory nations to tightly control the manufacture of drugs including opium, morphine and cocaine along with their derivatives. It allowed limited export and import of these substances under very strict regulations (Geneva Convention 1933).
>
> (ibid.: 46)

In 1950, there were a number of meetings for the control of drugs. Here, European countries were not any more emphatically against the US prohibitionist posture as they were at the beginning of the century. The main differences were now between the US and Europe and the producing countries (such as Turkey and Iran) (Rodrigues, 2003). It is in this context that Stimson (1994: 314) comments, 'imagine the response if the Pakistan government sent emissaries here to persuade our distillers to stop producing whisky because whisky drinking was causing a social problem in Pakistan'.

It is relevant to highlight that after the Second World War, there was a period of new pharmaceutical technologies and drug developments, such as antibiotics, vaccines, birth control pills and psychotropic drugs. Here, psychotropic drugs, as anti-psychotics and antidepressants, came to the market as consumer goods (Herzberg, 2009).

It was during the 1950s and 1960s that psychotropic drug therapies, 'happy-pills', flourished (ibid.). Moncrieff (2008) points out that, from the 1950s onwards, psychiatric drugs came to be viewed as specific substances for specific aims, reversing or treating abnormal brain states, and crediting the drugs for psychiatric cure and hope. This contrasts to an earlier model, drug-centred, in which drugs were seen as inducing abnormal states, producing sedation or stimulation. This new view and promises of cure were important for the establishment of psychiatry and pharmaceutical industries. In 1951, it was established that the Food and Drug Administration should be responsible for licensing substances for indications that medical experts suggested for treatment of diseases (Healy, 1997).

Although a number of physicians (see Healy, 2004; Moncrieff, 2008) contest the widespread psychiatric diagnosis – the way that depression has been massively diagnosed, the over-prescription of psychiatric drugs, inaccuracy of scientific research, drug trials in the case of depression (and other diagnosis), and the relations between pharmaceutical companies and medical practice (Healy, 2004) – this model is still central to contemporary psychiatry and medicine. Further, the category 'stimulants' was changed to 'antidepressants' in 1963, and in 1980 the mental illness of depression was included in the DSM-III. Moncrieff (2008: 2352) highlights that 'concept of the antidepressant helped to fashion our modern notion of depression'.

The attitude of intolerance regarding specific drugs was well established by the 1920s, and this approach remained until the 1950s. Drug policies were mainly based on the idea of fearfulness, and campaigns would depict drugs to be as dangerous as possible in an attempt to deter yung people from trying them. Here, specific social stereotypical images were promoted. Consequently, policy was built on and underlined these social stereotypes, as Campbell (2000: 12) points out:

> Drug policy provides a case study of the interplay between political power, knowledge production, and a parade of fantastic figures – the 'morphinist mothers' and 'opium vampires' of the nineteenth and early twentieth centuries, the 'enemies within' and the 'girl drug addict' of the 1950s, the 'heroin mothers' of the 1970s, and the 'crack moms' of more recent memory.

Prevalent cultural images connected to women played an important role in relation to discourses of drugs, promoting two polarised imaginaries: that of the victim and the threat. The white woman addict was an 'exotic' character; the opium vampire contrasted with the innocent childlike woman. Hence, the image of the vampire meets with that of the addict that flirts with death (Zieger, 2008). Stories that addiction could be spread, and the danger accorded to women, can be seen in the understanding that children should not stay with addicted mothers because they could contaminate them, or that boys should beware of women who could seduce them and pass on addiction, as depicted in the popular book *Opium: The Demon Flower*, published in 1926 (Campbell, 2000).

It is interesting to note these images of drugs and women in the contexts of the movies broadcast at that time. From 1934, drugs were banned in films. This lasted until 1948, when there was a relaxation of this law with the movie *To the Ends of the Earth*, which portrays the Federal Bureau of Narcotics stopping drug smuggling (Musto, 1999). Within this context, 'exploitation movies' of the 1930s and 1940s depicted drug use based on sensationalism, fear and exaggeration. Exploitation movies focused on sensational themes, such as drug abuse, prostitution, venereal disease and crime. These films are regarded as being responsible for the survival of independent movie theatres across the US (Feaster and Wood, 2002). Some examples of exploitation movies themed around drugs are *Reefer Madness*, *Marijuana*, *Cocaine Fiends* and *Narcotic*.

Reefer Madness (1938) is the most infamous of exploitation films.[1] It shows teenagers partying, and when taking marijuana they turn into homicidal maniacs, and the women become sexually uncontrollable and psychologically disturbed. The preface for the film anticipates it, I highlight some passages of the introduction to the movie: 'To sufficiently emphasise the frightful toll of the new drug menace which is destroying the youth of America in alarmingly increasing numbers. *Marihuana* is that drug – a violent narcotic – an unspeakable scourge – the real public enemy. Number One!' And further: 'The scenes and incidents, while fictionalised for the purpose of this story, are based upon *actual research* [my emphasis] into the results of Marihuana addiction.' After this introduction, the movie asks for action: 'Something *must be done* to wipe out this ghastly menace'. 'The dread *Marihuana* may be reaching forth next for your son or daughter . . . or *yours* . . . or YOURS!'

Narcotic (1933) tells the story of a doctor who, after a night in Chinatown, becomes a slave of opium. *Narcotic* also shows a picture of a man injecting drugs into a blonde woman. As Campbell (2000: 14) points out, 'another story attributed white women's fascination with the drug to curiosity'.

Another example of the portrayal of women and drugs is found in *Cocaine Fiends* (1936), a movie about a girl who is lured to the city because of cocaine. It tells of the degradation of drugs, and what can happen to those who submit to them, such as prostitution and immoral activities (Feaster and Wood, 2002).

Marihuana (1934) again shows a woman heroin addict, who 'aptly named Burma gave birth, lost her husband, and became the "ice queen of the snow peddlers" by selling headache powders to society matrons' (Campbell, 2000: 75). Interestingly, although the name of the movie

Figure 3.1 Marihuana (1934).

is *Marihuana*, the character is a heroin addict, bringing other discursive aspects into play.

These representations evoke the victimisation of women, and their moral degradation. Campbell (ibid.: 75) suggests that these movies 'positioned addicted white women as relays between the underworld and the "straight" world, between civilisation and its discontents'. These examples of the social imaginary of women and drugs still play a role in contemporary discourses of drugs, as I further elaborate in Chapter 6.

During the 1940s in the US, the image of drug users as 'enemy aliens' reinforced the connection between drugs and the two main deviant elements in this historical context: the sexual and the racial. Within the context of the Second World War, in the USA there was a fear that the Japanese could smuggle opium into the US, suggesting a 'new form of chemical warfare' (ibid.: 64). Later in the 1950s and 1960s, the threat of drugs extended to Russia, Asia and China: 'communism menaced modern democracy with "brainwashing" or "Pavlovian mind control" achieved through drugs' (ibid.: 64). By identifying the enemies, the US was discursively positioned as a victim nation, as Campbell (ibid.: 64) suggests:

> Both atavistic and futuristic constructions positioned the U.S. as a 'victim nation', which failed to explain why the nation was the world's most voracious drug consumer. Justifying why the US was the nation best suited to direct the global restriction of narcotics required the figure of an 'other'.

Hence, research and social policies were embedded within this context, (re)producing specific racialised and gendered imaginaries. Further, homosexuality, seen as deviant, was also prevalent in these associations. At the meeting of the American Psychiatric Association in 1934, marijuana was regarded as:

> A primary stimulus to the impulsive life with direct expression in the motor field. [It] releases inhibitions and restraints imposed by society and allows individuals to act out their drives openly [and] act as sexual stimulant [particularly to] overt homosexuals.
>
> (Musto, 1999: 220)

It is relevant to point out this connection between sexual stimulation and drugs, and the connection with homosexuality (double deviance), as it appears in other contexts and historical periods. In 1978, in the *Congresso Latino-Americano de Farmacologia*, a book was distributed called *Marihuana*: *Yerba Maldita* (Marihuana: Malevolent Herb) (see Masur and Carlini, 1993: 85):

> Marihuana and Homosexualism. What about a combination between homosexual and addicted (*viciado*) to marihuana. Unfortunately, many homosexuals are great consumers of narcotics and marihuana. And under its action they commit the most evil crimes against the individual and the integrity of his sex, without the boundaries of age, time and place. Marihuana, with its intoxicating effects and narcotics, allows them to spread their effect to adolescents, who incite them to smoke the plant, and once addicted (*viciado*) to the herb, they are obliged to be concubines. The adolescent with marihuana and stimulated towards homosexualism starts dressing up outrageously and wearing improper clothes for their gender.

This example highlights the connection between drug use and homosexuality, making explicit the threat of drug use: slavery and sexual release. Here, the threat to teenagers is clearly stated.

I have emphasised the medical and legal approaches to drugs, however it is relevant to point out that, in some contexts, some religious groups disapprove of the use of drugs, as well as homosexuality ('*For the bible tells me so*', 2007, Karslake), and some particular neo-evangelic groups promote sessions of exorcism against drug users and homosexual people, as revealed in the US and Brazil.

Contemporary discourses of drugs: drug policies

Public policies around drugs often oscillate between punishment and treatment according to political manoeuvres and public opinion about drugs and drug users. These policies are related to specific social and political contexts, where gender, class, race, age, sexuality and types of drugs are crucial to be accounted for. In this section, some examples of drug policies are highlighted. Drug policies regarding female drug users will be explored in Chapter 7.

It is important to highlight that, in terms of international drug policies, in general countries follow the guidelines established by the UN, although specific policies are developed in their own context (e.g. Brazil, see Rodrigues, 2003; Machado and Miranda 2007). Further, similarities between the images of drugs and drug users (and associations of race, gender and class) and consequent drug policies are seen in many Western countries.

During the 1960s, there was an increase in drug use in the UK and the US. Within the context of counter-culture, drug use had a different understanding by some groups, while the moral panic around drugs was heightened and the parameters of offence extended. The use of marijuana by the youth produced a gap between those who believed marijuana could turn them into 'maniacs' and those who used it without this aftermath, and, as a consequence of this, the youth mistrusted the warnings about drugs. At this time, there were a number of campaigns and shocking news about drugs in circulation. Another group that was targeted was the working class (Dally, 1996).

Despite the increase in drug use, the social climate around drugs was oscillating, as noticeable in the drug policies and laws deliberated in the US. Approaches in drug policies varied from more tolerance (less punishment and more treatment) to complete intolerance (as in the Reagan government).

In 1961 at the UN Convention in New York, the US was concerned with the eradication of heroin and cocaine worldwide. The convention established that states should increase control over legal drugs for medical use, and fight against drug traffic and illegal use.

During this period of counter-culture, some people favoured hallucinogenic drugs, such as LSD and marijuana, and the US started to tackle this group of drugs. An example is the pressure for the UN Convention of 1961 to include the amendment in 1972 including drugs that were not stated in 1961. The classification became: list 1 – hallucinogenic drugs, list 2 – amphetamines, lists 3 and 4 – different types of barbiturates. Only the drugs of list 1 were completely forbidden because they believed there was no medical use for these drugs. In 1972, Nixon declared the war on drugs (Rodrigues, 2003). Here, it is recognised and established that certain countries are considered producers and consumers, locating the US in a particular victim position – drugs coming from outside jeopardising the American youth, hence vilifying developing countries. Hence, this classification does not relate to the quality of the substance, but from utility to danger (abuse and dependency) (Lenson, 1995).

Musto (1999) argues that, if drugs were tackled according to their 'dangerousness', alcohol and tobacco should be on the list. Nevertheless, due to economic and powerful interests, alcohol and tobacco were not greatly feared. The first Federal Strategy for Drug Abuse and Drug Traffic Prevention (1973) tackled these substances, but stated that the target should first be 'illicit' drugs, whereas alcohol and tobacco were an important part of the social rituals and habits in the US.

In 1974, the US extinguished the Bureau of Narcotics and Dangerous Drugs (former bureau of Drug Abuse Control, from 1966–1968) and created the Drug Enforcement Agency, changing the name again to the Drug Enforcement Administration (DEA) (Rodrigues, 2003).

Methadone maintenance became established in anti-drug programs during Nixon's administration in the 1970s. This program formed a certain negotiation between tolerance with drug use and restriction of crime associated with heroin. So, drug users were offered something for their craving, although not their first choice. Here, although there was support for law enforcement (i.e. to cut off the foreign supply of heroin), the budget for treatment was larger (Musto, 1999). Moreover, it is interesting to note that, during the Vietnam War, a large number of soldiers were using opium (smoking) and more than 80 per cent were offered opium on their first arrival. However, on their return to the US, most of them would stop the use of the drug during the first year without treatment (Royal College of Psychiatrists, 2000; Tracy and Acker, 2004).

During the Carter government (late 1970s), there was a more tolerant approach to drug issues. It was said that 'penalties against possession of a drug should not be more damaging to an individual than the use of the drug itself; and where they are, they should be changed' (Musto, 1999: 261). This context is clear in the laws against marijuana possession for private use. Nevertheless, this is not related to decriminalisation, but rather tolerance to small amounts, and treatment was promoted rather than imprisonment.

During the 1980s, with the Reagan government, intolerance towards drugs was reinstated. It emphasised the reduction of availability rather than treatment (with the 'national crusade against drugs'). Drug tests were implemented in workplaces, and the motto 'just say no' was employed. This social policy was followed by the 'zero tolerance' campaign of the Bush administration, including the anti-drug abuse act of 1988, in which alcohol was included with other drugs. It was officially declared the 'war on drugs'. From this 'war on drugs', there was pressure on Latin American and other countries to stop coca growing (Musto, 1999).

From tolerance (1978) to reaction in the 1980s, increasingly drugs and drug users came to be perceived as a threat to US life and values. These discourses around drugs and drug users can be seen in changes in public discussion around these issues, and in official regulations governing proper vocabulary in government publications on drug abuse. It is important to point out a new association during this period – that of crack cocaine with African American people.

From 1969 to the early 1980s, there was an increase in cocaine powder use mainly among white people, and after the death of public figures and the emergence of crack cocaine, cocaine came to be seen as particularly addictive and dangerous. As a result of the non-tolerance approach, by 1990 the US had a population of 1.2 million prisoners sentenced for non-violent, drug-related crime (Royal College of Psychiatrists, 2000).

During the 1980s in Britain, heroin was portrayed as a drug for white and Asian people, while African Caribbean people were more typically associated with cannabis and crack cocaine, stereotypically linked with violence, 'loose living', social pathology, poor parenting, low education, poverty and single motherhood. Murji (1999) argues that the association with marijuana gave the police excessive powers to search young black men.

In the 1980s in the US, intolerance towards drugs was widespread, alongside the connection with minorities. For example, the anti-drug abuse act of 1986 established a scale of mandatory minimum sentences for cocaine offences based on the amount of powder or crack cocaine. The amounts were: 5 grams of crack cocaine or 500 grams of cocaine – from 5 to 40 years imprisonment, which could not be suspended, nor could the convict be paroled or placed on probation. This act appeared during a time of great fear and public disapproval of drugs, and the emergence of AIDS. In practice, there were more black offenders than white. The US Sentencing Commission explained in the 1997 special report to the congress:

> While there is no evidence of racial bias behind the promulgation of this federal sentencing law, nearly 90 per cent of the offenders convicted in federal court for crack cocaine distribution are African-American while the majority of crack cocaine users are white. Thus, sentences appear to be harsher and more severe for racial minorities than others as a result of this law. The current penalty structure results in a perception of unfairness and inconsistency.
>
> (Musto, 1999: 274)

The Sentencing Commission's 1997 Annual Report shows:

- federal defendants for LSD – 97 per cent white people;
- methamphetamine – 66 per cent white people;
- crack cocaine – 86 per cent black people;
- powdered cocaine – 48 per cent Hispanic people, 30 per cent black people, 21 per cent white people.

In 1997, during the Clinton administration, the mandatory minimum sentence for crack and cocaine changed, for crack 25 grams to 75 grams and cocaine 125 grams to 375 grams (Musto, 1999). Dorn and Lee (1999) emphasise that, in the US, the groups most likely to receive aggressive enforcement are minorities (African Americans, Hispanics), as well as low-income residents, and the low educated.

Dorn and Lee (ibid.) critically analyse the social policy of zero tolerance, pointing out that, by its nature, the target is on people rather than on addressing underlying problems. As McDonald (1994) argues, the notion of addiction as a crime, as a vice or a disease is in constant debate, and these approaches support each other. The emphasis on each approach will vary according to what the social and political context requires.

Further, the impact of the emergence of AIDS in drug policies is relevant to be highlighted, as more campaigns for homosexual people and women (also prostitution) appeared (as possible transmitters). It is important to highlight the discursive association between homosexuality, drug use and HIV, and their effects, such as the stigmatisation of homosexual people (Prado and Machado, 2008).

It was in this context that harm reduction initiatives gained importance in the early 1990s, targeting transmission of HIV by injecting practices, contrasting to previous drug policy campaigns on absenteeism. Harm reduction aims at decreasing drug use and the harm related to drug use (including alcohol and cigarettes). The main rationales for harm reduction are pragmatism, human rights, public health, focus on harm and dialogue, and drug users are seen as part of the larger community (Des Jarlais, 1995; Inciardi and Harrison, 2000; International Harm Reduction Association (IHRA), 2010, now called Harm Reduction International).

Harm reduction was highly debated, particularly by those who feared that needle exchange could induce drug use, and the US was more resistant to incorporate this form of policy (Inciardi and Harrison, 2000). A range of research has pointed out the importance of this approach for public health, for example on the effectiveness of strategies such as needle exchange and methadone maintenance 'in reducing transmission of infectious diseases and the deaths that these diseases cause' (Hunt and Stevens 2004: 335). This drug policy was first developed in the UK, the Netherlands and the US during the 1980s, aiming to reduce HIV transmission by intravenous use of drugs. The UK was prominent in harm reduction centres (e.g. Merseyside) in a context of increasing intravenous use of drugs. The first conference of harm reduction was held in Liverpool in 1990 (Harm Reduction International, 2011).

For harm reduction of psychiatric drugs, some self-organised groups of patients and survivors of psychiatric treatment (as they self-refer), together with professionals, organise meetings, conferences and publications providing information about psychiatric drugs, how to come out of them, indication of best practice clinics and self-help groups. In this context, I highlight in England the work of Asylum who produce *Asylum: The Magazine for Democratic Psychiatry* (www.asylumonline.net), which, since 1986, has struggled against psychiatrisation and stigmatisation, and has provided important information and space for users' voices (www.discourseunit.com). A series of networks were organised that challenged mainstream psychiatric views and for providing support, such as Survivors Speak Out and, in the 1990s, the National Self-Harm Network (feminist influence), Mad Pride, the Hearing Voices (Gordo-López 2002) and, more recently, the Paranoia Network (Parker, 2007).

In the UK, classification follows the international guidelines. The two main regulatory acts are the Misuse of Drugs Act (1971) and the Medicines Act (1968). The Misuse of Drugs Act control drugs for non-medical use, classifying them as class A (non-medical drugs, higher penalties for possession and supply and production), B (marihuana is now class b) and C. There are law changes when some drugs are reclassified (e.g. marijuana from B to C then B again), and inclusion of new drugs, and new uses of drugs (e.g. medical drugs used for non-medical reasons). For medical use, drugs are divided in schedules 1, 2, 3, 4 and 5, restricting the use of certain drugs for research only, use under prescription or medical use without prescription (available in pharmacies). The Medicines Act divides the supply of medicine into categories 1, 2 and 3: prescription only medicines, pharmacy medicines and general sales medicines.

In the UK in 1998, the government designed the strategy *Tackling Drugs to Build a Better Britain*, aiming at both law enforcement and drug prevention, a strategy set up between different groups and agencies, targeting young people, communities, treatment and availability. The Crime and Disorder Act (1998), tackling drug-related crime, and the Drugs Act (2005) were instated, including compulsory testing and/or treatment in connection to offences committed (DrugScope, 2011). Their main aim was to reduce offending using treatment to tackle substance misuse.

Researchers have pointed out the importance of these acts (Stimson, 2000; Hunt and Stevens, 2004), configuring a shift in the approach from health to crime, and drugs seen as 'engine of crime' (ibid.: 334). Earlier to this approach, concern was turned to the relation between drug use and HIV infection, understanding the drug user at risk of being harmed, and a risk to society by increasing diseases, particularly injecting drug users. The focus now is not on harm for the drug user, but rather drug use is now linked to crime and harming others (ibid.). McSweeney *et al.* (2006) point out that these measures are imposing greater restrictions to low-risk offenders, and enforcement of penalties is contributing to the increase in the number of detainees.

The shift of attention to crime is seen in the new acts on compulsory and quasi-compulsory drug treatment that have been enforced in the UK and US, and in other countries (the Netherlands, Germany and Brazil, among others). Drug courts were first developed in the US and partially informed the development of DTTOs (drug treatment and testing orders) (Hunt and Stevens, 2004). Researchers express concern about compulsory and quasi-compulsory treatment, regarding ethics, human rights and the effectiveness of these measures and treatment (Hunt and Stevens, 2004; McSweeney *et al.*, 2006).

Further, more recently drug policies are increasingly targeting alcohol and tobacco. After November 1989, all containers of beverage alcohol sold in the US should bear the message:

> GOVERNMENT WARNING: (1) According to the Surgeon General, women should not drink alcoholic beverages during pregnancy because of the risk of birth defects. (2) Consumption of alcoholic beverages impairs your ability to drive a car or operate machinery, and may cause health problems.
>
> (Musto, 1999: 277)

During the past years, measures have also been taken to tackle cigarette smoking in Western countries. The main discursive argument is related to self-harm and harming others, representing a shift in the approach to cigarette consumption. The basic measures of the regulation have taken the forms of 'bans and restrictions on advertising, strict package-labelling requirements, tort litigation against manufacturers, restrictions on engaging in the activity at work or even at home or while pregnant' (Gostin, 1997: 331), informing a newly emerging social imaginary of this drug and smokers.

The main argument for restricting smoking places is related to passive smoking. However, Gostin (ibid.) argues that the scientific conclusions presented in the surgeon general's report on involuntary smoking were less rigorous than in previous reports. In this report, the main conclusion was that involuntary smoking was a cause of disease, such as lung cancer. These studies established a causal connection in certain cases. Nevertheless, the report failed to state clearly the conditions to create a significant health risk; more specifically, at what level of exposure the risk occurs, such in the case of mild or intermittent exposure.

In 2003, the World Health Organization organised the first international treaty on public health, the WHO framework convention on tobacco control, which required countries to impose restrictions on the production, advertisement and distribution of cigarettes. This act is believed to have had a profound impact on the laws and policies regarding tobacco. However, at that time, countries such as the US, Germany and China (as well as Brazil, among others) made it clear that many parts of the act could not be followed. These countries consume 40 per cent of cigarettes worldwide. This act aims to regulate the consumption of smoking by prohibiting under 18s to smoke, to adopt legislation and political action against black market, a ban on any kind of advertisement for 5 years, an increase in cigarette taxation, the acknowledgement of the responsibility for diseases caused by cigarettes (cigarette manufacturers and government), at least 30 per cent of cigarette packets should have a warning message (such as 'smokers die younger'), and the need to tackle women, young girls and indigenous people's consumption. In Chapter 5, I examine the moral perspective embedded in discourses of smoking.

In relation to drug policy, I stress here the importance of taking into account the differences in drug consumption and types of drugs according to specific social and historical contexts, considering gender, sexuality, class, race and age, and the different forms of consumptions and types of drugs. For example, in Brazil, consumption of drugs such as marijuana, amphetamines, inhalants and anxiolytics is not very different from international consumption, that is, around 20 to 35 per cent, with the exception of the US, which is 96.6 per cent (COTRIM, 1991 in Bucher, 1992). In this research, it was pointed out that at that time the psychoactive substances most consumed among students were first solvents, then medical drugs (anxiolytics and amphetamines), and third marijuana. Thus, the specific context and types of drugs are crucial for the analysis, and, as known, there were very few (if any) campaigns targeting solvents in Brazil. Further, this example also points out the need to review what are considered drugs, as these two groups of drugs, solvents and psychotropic medical drugs, are usually not considered drugs for the drug policies.

The focus on the consumption of medical drugs reveals that, in debates around drugs, these substances are often neglected or at times not considered 'drugs'. Yet, in the UK and US, there is a considerable increase in the consumption of these drugs, as Illich (1995: 69) notes:

> In England, every tenth night of sleep is induced by a hypnotic drug and 19 per cent of women and 9 per cent of men take a prescribed tranquilliser during any one year. In the United States, central-nervous-system agents are the fastest growing sector of the pharmaceutical market, now marking up 31 per cent of total sales.

Other research (Moore *et al.*, 2009: 1) also point to an increase in antidepressant prescriptions in the UK (as well as in Australia and Canada). They highlight quoting Prescription Pricing Authority that prescribing 'increased by 36 per cent to 7.3 million items per quarter between 2000 and 2005'. Further, the report highlights that cases of depression among young women increased between 1993 and 2005 and that, in general, women are more diagnosed with depression than men. In this direction, studies have highlighted international trends of higher use of psychotropic drugs by women and the elderly, and lower socio-economic groups, which are more prescribed (Ettorre and Riska, 1995; Cooperstock and Parnell, 2002). In 2010, the United Nations

Commission on Narcotic Drugs expressed concern over the use of prescription drugs.

In this sense, it is also crucial to consider how gender, race, class and age operate for distinct forms of consumption of drugs recreationally and medically. Further, in previous research, over-prescription of antidepressants to some groups of asylum seekers in the UK has been identified (Dawson, 2003), as well as the need to research this over-prescription to women asylum seekers (Mountian, 2005b).

Regarding generation, Lopes (1999) comments on the high prescription of tranquillisers and hypnotics for elderly people, where women comprise the largest percentage of consumers worldwide. Despite this, Lopes argues that emotional changes are not necessarily higher in the elderly group, while the side effects of these products are in fact greater for elderly people.

These examples are the subject of another debate that cannot be discussed in depth here, but point to interrogating the practice of some doctors over-prescribing psychiatric drugs to non-dominant groups (considering age, gender, class, race), the greater social pressures on these groups, and how drugs can function as a form of social control. Ettorre and Riska (1995) highlight the gender bias and one-dimensional research conducted, so that, although the use of tranquillisers is seen as an emergent social problem, the analysis should account for the structural inequalities that produce these problems for women.

Regarding drug use worldwide, a number of reports have pointed out that, despite efforts in the direction of drug control and punishment, consumption of illegal drug use has in fact increased (for the UK, see Birdwell *et al.*, 2011) and a number of new drugs have been produced (ibid.). Studies (ibid.) point out that traditional drug control and enforcement should be reviewed, as users may be exposed to dangerous substances, and that the effects of this legislation can be more harmful to the individual than the drugs themselves (Inciardi and Harrison, 2000). Reports also highlight the need for more research into the new drugs, and how policy makers ignore possible benefits of drugs, which may play a role in the decision to use drugs (Reuter, 2011). The Internet and global market is also seen as changing drug habits (ibid.).

From these key points of the contemporary history of drugs, two aspects are emphasised here: how drug policy regarding laws and treatment represents and shapes discourses around drugs, where societal values and ideologies on the nature of addiction tend to determine the thrust and content of government policy, and how laws are intimately connected to medical research. It is a claim that is fundamental to consider the social context of drug use.

Drug policy of war on drugs

International prohibition did not stop the production and sale of psychoactive substances, but rather it increased law enforcement, state apparatus and illegal market. Some reports (McSweeney *et al.*, 2008) suggest that drug dealing is the most profitable criminal activity in the UK. Studies highlight the problems of the creation of a universal law that does not account for the local cultures and specificities (Rodrigues, 2003), and as such a number of effects of prohibition have been highlighted (Karam, 2008; Reuters and Stevens, 2007), such as, violence, repression, misinformation, lack of drug quality control and health hazard for users (information, drug quality, risk of contamination from diseases such as HIV and hepatitis).

Further, the specificity of the war on drugs should be further researched. As Rodrigues (2003, 2004) highlights, the relation between prohibition and the emergence of drug trafficking forms a war that involves estates, drug business, armed groups and social forces, compounding a specific type of war. As already mentioned, the US has been the leader in the crusade against drugs (Rodrigues, 2003). Moreover, Labrousse (2010) discusses the geopolitics of drugs, highlighting that three quarters of illicit drugs (cocaine, opium and cannabis) are planted, different from synthetic drugs, thus changing the type of sale and requirements of production. The psychoactive substances that are planted are largely produced in the developing world, bringing another set of issues.

This chapter has focused on key events in the history of drugs, emphasising the medical and legal classification of drugs, the religious (moral), ideological component embedded in these spheres, and imaginaries that these discourses evoke, focusing on particular intersections between gender, race and class, identifying the primitivising, orientalising and sexualising discourses around drugs.

Furthermore, while medical and legal definitions of drugs are, at times, ambiguous and contradictory, they play a fundamental role in contemporary notions of drugs and addiction. These ambiguities inform the discussion on the moral and ethical standpoints of discourses of drugs in the next chapter.

4 Discourses of addiction

In Chapter 3, I highlighted key events in the history of drugs, and identified medical, legal and religious discourses on drugs as having a major impact on the mainstream social imaginary of drugs. The signifier 'drug' was indicated as discursively operating according to broader social, political and cultural contexts while it also informs and reflects societal values and practices.

The definition of drugs was highlighted as related to specific practices of consumption. Three aspects have been identified: (1) the creation of a specific social imaginary of drugs and drug users (considering gender, class and race); (2) the medical, legal and religious approaches to drugs and their intersections; and (3) the emergence of the disease theory of addiction that forms the focus for this chapter.

Here, I draw on the notion of *pharmakon*, and critically analyse medical and religious discourses on drug addiction, the understanding of health as an ethics of life, hierarchical moral dichotomies evoked by these discourses, and the debate between the concept of addiction and free will.

Etymology of drugs

The etymology of the words 'drugs' and 'addiction' allows a more descriptive approach to these terms. There is some controversy on the etymology of the word drug (*drogia* in Latin, *daruk* in Iran, *durâwa* in Arabic and *druko* for Celts). The most accepted is the Middle Dutch word *droghe vate*, meaning 'barrel of dry goods' (Vargas, 2008), used in the context of the early spice trade between the West and the East. Looking at the meanings attached to the word, drugs, in this sense, did not carry negative connotations. This same relation can be seen in names for other drugs, such as 'opium' from the Greek *opos*, the juice of a plant, 'alcohol' from the Arabic *al-kuhl*, meaning 'a fine dry powder', and Paracelsus' use of the expression alcohol *vini* for 'the essence of the wine' (Zoja, 1989).

Escohotado (1998) argues that, when a moral connotation was applied to drugs, narcotics lost the clarity of pharmacological definition. From the Greek *narkoun*, meaning to sleep, or to sedate, these substances produce specific effects, however they came to refer to all kinds of drugs. 'In the context of international drug control, "narcotic drug" means any drug defined as such under the 1961 Convention' (Laboratory and Scientific Section United Nations Office on Drugs and Crime, 2003: 77).

Hence, it is relevant to note that the use of the word 'drug 'as equivalent to narcotics had met resistance (by pharmacists) because of its misleading and loose meaning, and also due to the discursive connection between illegal drugs and narcotics (Parascandola, 1996), as in mainstream discourses, 'narcotics' came to be seen as 'nasty', 'dangerous' or 'illegal' substances (Dally, 1996).

Pharmakon

The notion of remedy is of major importance for the understanding of medical discourses of drug use. As religious discourses differentiate sacred substances ('plants of power') from drugs, medical discourses distinguish remedies from drugs, thus these differentiations are related to the forms of consumption of specific substances. In the notion of *remedy*, there is an attempt to isolate certain qualities of a drug, related to a specific form of use. Derrida (1997), elaborating on the ambivalent character of *pharmakon*, emphasises the notion of 'remedy' in which there is an attempt to associate only virtue to the substance:

> As opposed to 'drug' or even 'medicine', remedy says the transparent rationality of science, technique, and therapeutic causality, thus excluding from the text any leaning toward magic virtues of a force whose effects are hard to master, a dynamics that constantly surprises the one who tries to manipulate it as master and as subject.
>
> (Derrida, 2000 [1972]: 99)

Here, the positivistic framework of medicine is highlighted, in which a causal relation is the basis of this rationale. However, these qualities cannot be separated. Derrida (1997) indicates that it is not possible to distinguish remedy from poison, as well as good from evil, truth from falsity, the inside from the outside, the vital from the mortal.

Escohotado (1998) argues that, in fact, psychopharmacology exemplifies this conflict: on the side of the good, there are innumerable therapeutic and playful uses, related to the need of euphoria and good mood (*anima*). On the side of the evil, there is the rejection of inconveniences, such as the individual risk of severe and chronic intoxication.

Focusing on the word *pharmakon*, which in Greek means at the same time both medicine and poison, it is possible to discuss the quality of good and evil as contained within the substance. Derrida (1997) highlights that this 'medicine', this filter, which is at the same time remedy and poison, is introduced to the body of discourse with all its ambivalence. It carries a quality of fascination and power of enchantment that can be alternating or simultaneously good or evil.

In this sense, *pharmakon* is a substance that includes everything that this word connotes concerning its material, its hidden virtues, its cryptic depth, and its ambivalence that defies analyses. Derrida suggests that, in this sense, it is possible to acknowledge *pharmakon* as the proper anti-substance, 'that which resists any philosopheme, indefinitely exceeding its bounds as non-identity, nonessence, nonsubstance' (Derrida, 2000 [1972]: 75), and for this very reason it provides the infinite adversity of its depth and lack of depth.

The 'essence' of *pharmakon* is that of not having a stable essence, neither unique character, nor being in any sense of the word (metaphysical, physical, chemical or alchemical) a substance. The *pharmakon* does not have any ideal identity. The non-identity of the *pharmakon*, as conceived according to a philosophical perspective, gives some insights about the complexity of its definition. This meets the previous elaboration (in Chapter 3) on Heidegger's (1997) notion of equipment, in which there is no such a thing as equipment, but rather equipment is always in order-to. In this sense, drugs are constructed according to the use in specific contexts. Here, it is possible to ask: what are the qualities attached to *pharmakon*? How does this flexibility of *pharmakon* operate within the drug field?

Addiction, habituation and dependence

The emphasis on the signifier 'addiction' is of major importance, as discourses on 'drugs' are strongly connected to addiction. Addiction, a notion largely based on medical assumptions, is a term broadly used (not only in relation to drugs), it permeates societal ideas about drug use, and is widely disseminated in research, media, public health policies and lay discourses.

It is interesting to note that, although the word 'addiction' is in widespread use, the scientific world has agreed to some extent to use the term 'drug dependence' as a replacement for addiction. Indeed, the World Health Organization (WHO) abandoned the terms 'addiction' and 'habituation' in 1964 in favour of 'drug dependence'. Moreover, WHO differentiates 'addiction' and 'abuse', based on the *Lexicon of Alcohol and Drug Terms* (WHO, 1994), as we shall see. Notwithstanding this, the use of the term 'addiction' still remains in medical research, health disciplines and health policies.

The terms indicating addiction came to carry negative connotations when these words became increasingly associated with the substances themselves. The German word *Sucht* refers to drug addiction in general. It comes from Old German and Gothic and has always meant 'illness'. The word 'addict' appears in England around the sixteenth century. It derives from the Latin *addictus*, 'handed over (to someone) as a slave' (Zoja, 1989). Zoja suggests that 'addiction' thus originally meant giving oneself over, but progressively the meaning became connected with the use of drugs. In the same vein, the verb 'to crave' comes from the Old Norse verb for 'to ask or demand intensely'.

Traditionally, the word 'addiction' has meant a strong inclination towards certain kinds of conduct with little or no pejorative meaning attached to it. Szasz (1975) notes some examples of the use of this term in the *Oxford English Dictionary* pre-twentieth century, which included being addicted to civil affairs, to useful reading and also to bad habits. However, being addicted to drugs was not among the definitions, and until quite recently, the term 'addiction' referred to a habit, good or bad. Although addiction still has this use, its meaning nowadays came to refer 'to almost any kind of illegal, immoral, or undesirable association with certain kinds of drugs' (ibid.: 6), and specific behaviours.

It was towards the end of the nineteenth century and the beginning of the twentieth century that the association between drug, abuse and addiction was established. From 1897, articles started to appear using the terms 'drug habits', 'drug addiction' and 'drug patients' (mainly in North American and British journals) (Parascandola, 1996). It is worth noting that the association between drugs and abuse became widespread after the First World War (see Chapter 3).

The definition of 'addiction' proposed by the World Health Organization (WHO) is that:

> Addiction refers to the repeated use of a psychoactive substance or substances, to the extent that the user is *periodically* or

> chronically intoxicated, shows a compulsion to take the preferred substance (or substances), has great difficulty in voluntarily ceasing or modifying substance use, and *exhibits determination to obtain psychoactive substances by almost any means*.
>
> (Laboratory and Scientific Section United Nations Office on Drugs and Crime, 2003: 73, my emphasis)

This definition contrasts with 'habituation', which means to become accustomed to any behaviour or condition.

This definition of addiction is not very precise, as it is not clear what levels of 'determination' are required, and it does not explain which 'means' constitute the experience of addiction. Further, discursively particular moral standpoints are identified, since they imply a specific mode of behaviour (e.g. *exhibits determination to obtain psychoactive substances by almost any means)*. These definitions have to be seen in particular contexts. Although this classification can be applied to any individual using any psychotropic drug for specific diseases, the ill person is often not regarded as an addict, so discursively they came to implicitly refer to illegal drug use. Szasz (1994) argues that the understanding of addiction referring to people who would go to 'any means' to obtain drugs carries a presupposition that addiction only occurs in relation to illegal substances or very expensive ones. This somehow implies a proper way of using drugs (e.g. with prescription for medical reasons), as opposed to the purpose of 'pharmacological pleasure', positioning such illicit pleasures within the realms of moral values and law.

Hence, these understandings of addiction are not neutral references to people's use of drugs. As Szasz (1975: 16) points out, 'in its descriptive sense, the term "addiction" tells us something about what the "addict" does to *himself*; in its ascriptive sense, it tells us something about what those making the judgement plan to do to *him*'.

This definition of addiction contrasts with habituation, which discursively implies a socially accepted use of drugs (Young, 1971). In fact, the notion of habit can be seen losing its place in drug debates. As Sedgwick (1992: 591) notes, 'the worldly concept of habit has dropped out of theorised use with the superinvention in this century of addiction and the other glamorising paradigms oriented around absolutes of compulsion/volition'.

For the UN definition, 'drug dependence' is as follows:

> It comprises a cluster of physiological, behavioural and cognitive phenomena of variable intensity, in which the use of a psychoactive

> drug (or drugs) takes on a high priority. It implies a need for repeated doses of the drug to feel good or avoid feeling bad'. 'Psychological or psychic dependence' refers to the experience of impaired control over drug use. 'Physiological or physical dependence' involves the development of *tolerance* and *withdrawal symptoms* upon cessation of use of the drug, as a consequence of the body's adaptation to the continued presence of a drug.
>
> (Laboratory and Scientific Section United Nations Office on Drugs and Crime, 2003: 74)

The Diagnostic and Statistical Manual of Mental Disorders (DSM), published by the American Psychiatric Association, and the Classification of Mental and Behavioural Disorders (ICD 10), published by WHO, define drug dependence in relation to physical and psychological dependence, and understand drug addiction as a mental illness.

In relation to the definition of dependency, this definition still is not very clear when it does not specify what dependency is. For example, what is 'high priority'? And moreover, in such definitions, the individual and social contexts are not taken into consideration, implying a specific use of drugs, drawing on the opposition between medical and recreational use.

The changes in language for drugs and addiction are indicative of the way that drugs are understood, and have an impact on the relationship between the object-drug and those who use them (White, 2004). Hence, addiction and dependency are notions that have to be located in their specific social and political contexts. Moreover, dependency is typically seen as an undesirable aspect of human behaviour, conceived as less natural, less 'healthy' or less satisfying, and commonly regarded as an undesirable quality. Drawing on Dean and Taylor-Gooby's (1992) discussion of the underclass and welfare dependency, the meanings evoked by 'dependency' can be seen to connote lack of power. The term is also highly gendered, with autonomy regarded as the cultural ideal of Western masculinity and dependence as attributed to the feminised 'other'.

Focusing on drug dependency, it is important to stress the moral connotation that this latter formulation brings out. As highlighted by McDonald (1994: 3), 'it is still the case that the imputed "addictiveness" of a substance holds a persuasive congruence with the degree of religious and political fear of it, and the capacity for evil attributed to it'. In this sense, even the use of the word 'chemical' is saturated by negative connotations, contrasting with discourses of the body as organic and natural (Keane, 1999), or pure. In this way, it is interesting to note the notions of natural and artificial as described by Irigaray (1989 in Frosh, 1995), in which the natural is seen as cyclical and organic, while artificial is labyrinthine, being therefore subjected to law, as is the case with drugs.

As previously mentioned, the focus solely on chemical effects restricts a broader understanding of drug use, isolating the substance from the social and individual contexts. As Gianesi (2002) puts it, it addresses the signification of the substances, isolating the signifier from its signification (i.e. the concrete effect of the chemical formulas).

Before proceeding further, it is important to reiterate at this point that the claim of this analysis is not to deny the experience of addiction. Rather, the objective is to analyse discourses of addiction and its applications. As Loose (2002b: 273) points out, drawing on the work of Zafiropoulos, 'addiction exists, but there is no such person as *the* (typical) addict'.

Addiction as disease

Addiction came to be seen as mental illness in contemporary medical literature. This notion has its basis on the disease theory that became widespread in the beginning of the twentieth century, bringing questions regarding social regulation and control to the fore. The disease theory of addiction played a fundamental role for the warranting of medical intervention.

The medical approach conceives of addiction primarily as a disease of the brain, in which medical explanations focus on the toxicology of drugs and their neurological effects, concerning personality change and physical effects (MacGregor, 1999). Contemporary UN reports define drug addiction as a chronic multifactorial health disorder, and 'largely a function of genetic heredity (United Nations Commission on Narcotic Drugs, 2010: 59). This approach does not account for the social and individual contexts.

It is important to highlight that not all therapeutic models approach addiction in the same way. For example, some schools of psychoanalysis have a distinct approach to drug addiction – they do not confine addiction to a pathology, rather they locate the relationship with the object-drug within the subject's discourse, based on a distinct psychoanalytic ethical perspective (Mountian, 2004a; Dunker, 2011; Neill, 2011; Parker, 2011; Rosa and Mountian, 2012).

Critical analysis of the disease theory reveals important aspects regarding the individual pathologisation and the moral components attached to the understanding of addiction as mental illness. As Illich (1995: 92) has noted, 'in the detection of sickness medicine does two things: it "discovers" new disorders, and it ascribes these disorders to concrete individuals'.

It is relevant to highlight the discursive effect of diagnosis as producing a security of knowing. As Loose (2002b) suggests, the nosology and classification of mental disorders secures the illusion of control and mastery over something that is unknown or not understood. However, this security is an illusion because the nosological names do not correspond to their empirical reality; but rather they obscure that reality. In the same vein, Keane (1999) points out that, although there is a belief that finding a diagnosis and aetiological factors will complete the understanding of the disease, this is in fact a masking tendency.

Keane *et al.* (2011) argue that, because this diagnosis is often for the already marginalised subjects, it can function as dismissing their demands and experience as valid, rather than taking them as pathological. This contrasts to other *legitimate* forms of addiction, such as the authors' comment, 'pseudoaddiction', an iatrogenic condition caused by medical treatment, described in pain medicine for 'disordered behaviour of patients who increase their dose without approval, complain aggressively or lie to obtain more drugs, and turn to street drugs or "doctor shopping"' (ibid.: 876).

The relationship between doctors and patients has been highlighted in previous studies (N. Rose, 1994; Illich, 1995; Young, 1971). Loose (2002b) suggests that one of the effects of the medical model is the position of dependency of the patient in relation to an authority, a 'master who knows', for example in institutions such as psychiatric asylums in which the 'chef de clinique' knows what is good for the patient. In this sense, 'treatment takes place within a discourse in which there is no place for the choices, desires and responsibilities of the subject' (ibid.: 268). This paradigm is juxtaposed with the reductionist materialistic model, in which psychopathology should have an organic cause.

Here, in both cases, the subject is an 'accidental' element of the therapeutic treatment that takes place despite his/her responsibility. In this sense, within the moral paradigm, the environment is responsible for the problem of the subject, while in the organicist paradigm, the subject is a victim of organic causes. These approaches do not allow any other subject position in discourse, rather than that of the victim. The position of victim is an important aspect of the disease theory. As described by Illich (1995: 168):

> Advanced industrial societies have a high stake in maintaining the epistemological legitimacy of disease. As long as disease is something that takes possession of people, something they 'catch' or 'get', the victims of these natural processes can be exempted from responsibility for their condition.

Taking up the organic approach of the disease theory of addiction, a range of discourses can be identified: addiction as something contagious, that can be caught, inherited addiction (genetic), or addiction as chemical dependency, which can also discursively function as legitimising the use of drugs (i.e. a real dependency, need). In this sense, discursively, addiction as a disease can release the drug user from responsibility over his/her use, since their use is the consequence of a disease, which implicitly requires an authority to cure it.

Young (1971: 89) suggests that this model in which the individual sees himself/herself as normal but having caught a disease is in some ways a successful strategy. In this strategy, 'there is no necessity for the individual to bifurcate himself; here, all his weakness is projected outside him on the "virus" of drug dependency, his self being seen as united and irreproachable in any part', the individual has taken the role that was allocated to him, that is, of the sick. Further, it is important here to consider how these discourses are utilised, either by doctors and patients, or the users themselves. Some resist this model, others adopt it and use it strategically, and some identify themselves with the position of the victim. This aspect is clear in the discourses of institutionalised drug users who utilise the same discourses to understand their conditions (Mountian, 2004b).

Indeed, N. Rose (1994: 64) identifies this dynamic by pointing out that the apparatuses of health (the medical administration of public and domestic space) rely on relations between experts and subjects. Each of these mechanisms embodies different practices of rights (of speaking, listening, prescribing and obeying) and these ways constitute the 'persona of the expert as a technician of health'. These discourses connect to specific images of the individual, and to the ways that they problematise their lives in the logic of health.

In the same vein, Illich (1995: 133) stresses the dependency of the sufferer on professional care and the production of a (morbid) society that urges universal medicalisation. In this kind of discourse, there is a belief that defining and diagnosing diseases is better than other forms of negative label or no label at all, which is preferable to discourses of criminality, political deviance, laziness, or self-chosen absence from work. 'The doctor functioning as a lawyer by exempting the patient from normal duties, and as a priest by creating the myth that he is a victim of biological mechanisms, rather than lazy or greedy'.

Although the medical model locates itself in a rather contrasting position to religious moralities, particularly when focusing on the physiological aspects of addiction, it still highlights paradoxical aspects of discourses of addiction and specific moral standpoints.

Free will

An important variant of discourses on addiction is structured around the notion of free will. Berridge and Edwards (1987) suggest that the element of free will and personal responsibility coexisted uneasily with the medical and scientific basis, being in illogical alliance also with the notion of psychological influence in disease theory. In order to bridge this gap between moral and medical perspectives, organic explanations of illness were utilised, including the idea that insanity (including addiction) had its source in localised brain lesions. In this way, variations in mental and moral characteristics were a function of physical defects.

McMurran (1994) distinguishes the religious (moral) and medical models (disease theory) and highlights that the moral approach for human behaviour is based on the notion of free will in which people are supposed to be able to choose what they will do in a variety of situations. However, behaviours that contravene social norms are seen as sinful, weak-willed, and/or as social nuisance. In such cases, responses to undesirable behaviour within this model would be religious counselling, legislative controls and punishment.

With regard to the medical model, McMurran (ibid.) suggests that the notion of free will gave way to determinism, in which every event, including human behaviour and thinking, should have a cause, and science would provide the explanations for these events. The most significant development was the application of medical concepts to problems that had previously been regarded within moral or spiritual domains (e.g. 'homosexualism' and drug use as mental illness).

In this way, undesirable behaviours came to be seen as symptoms for physical malfunctions and, in cases where there were no apparent physical causes, the notion of 'mental illness' was evoked. When undesirable behaviour was seen as a disease, treatment would be used rather than punishment, although some treatments carried some degree of punishment. Hence, approaches to deal with undesirable behaviours contain both moral and medical discourses: legislation (crime), religious morality (sin) and medical intervention (disease).

Although medicine was conceived of as an 'objective science', located in opposition to religious morality, medical discourses are not value-free. Rather, they are socially and historically situated, and (re)producing hierarchical moral dichotomies, such as natural/artificial, inside/outside, truth/falsity and public/private (Keane, 1999).

The notion of free will strongly figures within this debate, as addiction is commonly regarded as opposed to freedom, lack of power and control. The notions of free will, addiction and dependence need to be considered within their socially specific location, that is, by whom, and what type of free will can be chosen and freely expressed?

Free will is an exercise that is often praised in democratic societies. Nonetheless, some choices are not seen as free will, which is a logical paradox. 'The object of addiction is the exercise of those very qualities whose lack is supposed to define addiction as such: bodily autonomy, self-control, will power' (Sedgwick, 1992: 583).

The utilisation of medical terminologies in everyday language has become widespread. In the case of addiction, it came to connote behaviours that are seen as 'excessive, habitually repetitive, or problematic' (White, 2004: 42). Addiction is popularly used for behaviours of a compulsive sort regarding relations with a range of objects (e.g. psychoactive substances, food, gym, televisions, computer games, and including sex and people), and a number of behaviours are named after this understanding of addiction, such as sex addiction, workaholic, shopaholic, chocoholic, caffeine addiction, eating addiction, gym addiction.

Within this range of practices regarded as addictive, such as 'workaholism', 'shopaholism', 'sexual compulsiveness', and 'co-dependency' or 'relationship addiction', Sedgwick (1992: 584) comments that, 'as each assertion of will has made volition itself appear problematic in a new area, the assertion of will itself has come to appear addictive'.

Hence, the contemporary approach to addiction can diagnose any substance, behaviour or effect, as addictive, making the notion of free will central to the relationship between the body and the substance. In the case of drug addiction, the individual is said to be chemically controlled. Within this definition of addiction 'resides only in the structure of a will that is always somehow insufficiently free, a choice whose volition is insufficiently pure' (ibid.: 584).

The discursive argument on drug addiction states that people who are not addicted have more control over their behaviour than the addicts, therefore they are freer (Davies, 1997). This line of argumentation, which could be said to be reductionist, in being located only in opposition to non-addicts, brings forward some ethical and moral questions related to normative sanctions and risking pathologising individuals, producing the idea of the drug user as a victim.

Moreover, the addiction/free will opposition seems to propagate a specific idea of free will. Hence, this notion of free will is historically specific, also considering gender, class and race differences within social-political contexts. Usually, the concept is not challenged; rather, for the effectiveness of this signifier, it requires it to be spread, circulated and continually displaced. So, as free will is saturated with moral and ethical values, there will be 'compulsion' as its counterpart, internal to it and required to be renegade (Sedgwick, 1992).

In previous research (Mountian, 2004a), the question on control over the substance use was emphasised, and at times resisted, for the definition of addiction:

J: No, in this sense or reduction of choice, I don't recognise. Yeah, I mean, in my case, with the use of this specific drug [marijuana] I don't think so. It is perfectly of course that you keep yourself very present in these choices (. . .). I think that this is the contrary of this theory of addiction, because it is the exercise of will. It is the active exercise of will, an option, it is not a non-option.

D: Yeah, I use to enjoy myself, this though is the basic reason, there is this specific use. Ah, I mean the more hallucinogenic drugs. I use marijuana frequently, I have always at home, but I don't put myself, neither ever felt as dependent or addict, even cigarette that I smoke, I don't consider myself an addict (*viciada*), because my relationship with the thing, is very like, I determine, like this, the moment that I want to use, (. . .), if I want to.

These two examples point to a discourse of drugs where the subject controls their use. Here, the idea of loss of control is denied by both interviewees, who act according to their choices (free will), thus also resisting the position of 'addict'. These examples also point to a logical paradox for the notion of addiction and control.

A critical analysis of the signifier free will is crucial in drug discourses, particularly considering the ethical and moral values imbued with this concept and the historical and social context of free will. Crucially, behaviours that are seen as morally wrong (particularly body pleasures) are often taken as the subject's impossibility to choose – 'I can resist everything but temptation' (Wilde, 2007/1892). This is particularly problematic in terms of gender, with body pleasure for women still highly regarded as morally wrong, calling to question body autonomy.

Hierarchical moral dichotomies

With the widespread use of the term 'addiction', it is important to analyse the ethical and moral aspects evoked by such discourses, which often circulate around hierarchical discursive binaries: good and bad, organic and artificial, real and illusory, free will and addiction, dependency and control.

These discourses of drugs and addiction are directly concerned with legitimacy, based on the opposition between natural and artificial, true and false and pure and impure, discourses on drugs underline legitimate pleasures, legitimate free will. Sedgwick (1992: 589), drawing on *The Picture of Dorian Gray* and *Dr. Jekyll and Mr. Hyde* (erotic tension between men and solitary substance abusers) highlights how:

> The two new taxonomies of the addict and the homosexual condensed many of the same issues for late nineteenth-century culture: the old-anti-sodomitic opposition between something called 'nature' and that which is *contra naturam* blended with a treacherous apparent seamlessness into a new opposition between substances that are natural (for example, 'food') and those that are artificial (for example, 'drugs'), and hence into the characteristic twentieth century way of distinguishing desires themselves between the natural, called 'need', and the artificial, called 'addictions'.

The signifiers 'natural' and 'artificial', 'need' and 'addiction' reproduce specific moral and ethical standpoints, and are ultimately related to legitimacy. In fact, Keane (1999: 70), drawing on Derrida, points out that the attachment to pleasure is what is held against the drug user. The objection is not about the pleasure of the user *per se*, but, 'we cannot abide that this is a pleasure taken in an experience without truth'. In this sense, the neurological discourse provides grounds for the division between false and real pleasures, in which the inauthenticity of the drug addict is chemically produced and objectively verifiable.

Queer theory provides some further insights on debates of the legitimacy of body and pleasure, particularly on the relation of ethics to pleasure, the nature of consent, and the definition of freedom.

Warner (1999: 20) argues that 'sexual coercion and violence were justified in the name of national health'. If homosexuality and addiction are portrayed as medical conditions, this locates medicine as a specific strategy for legitimacy.

We can identify some further discursive moral dichotomies produced in drug discourses: such as artificial vs. natural, enjoyment vs. cure, dependency vs. control, free will vs. addiction, leisure vs. productivity, pleasure vs. need, true vs. false. Hierarchies among drugs can also be seen: illegal vs. legal, whisky vs. beer, marijuana vs. cigarettes, coffee vs. tea, drinking in the morning vs. drinking at the weekend, drinking alone vs. drinking with friends (gender plays an important role here, as seen in Chapter 6).

In the name of health

In the analysis of the moral dichotomies identified as evoked by medical discourses, specific forms of understandings of health emerge, which are situated understandings of the body, of behaviour and, moreover, of principles of life, establishing what is 'normal', so constituting and reproducing specific moral and ethical standpoints. Health is socially and politically located (in all senses, from the distribution of health to understandings of health).

Illich (1995) argues that medicine is conceived of as a moral enterprise when it gives content to good and evil, by defining what is normal, proper or desirable, as law and religion do. Medicine is not only related to cure, but inaugurates an ethics of living. In this sense, N. Rose (1994: 67) argues, 'our present is suffused with the ethic of the humanist, the ethic of the normal social person, which is intrinsically an ethic of the healthy body'. All aspects of care are related, therefore, to the logic of health, and organised in terms of normality.

In this sense, secular values of health may be seen discursively replacing the non-corporeal or theological virtues, becoming the main ethical approach, and constituting a 'new' morality. This secular morality prescribes behaviour and is related to a particular understanding of health (mental and physical) and fitness movement (Katz, 1997). Katz discusses this new kind of morality as supplementing the traditional moral code that deals with sin, and redemption from sin, constructed on many of the same principles. This new code operates as a complex syncretism of contemporary beliefs overlaying the old framework, where the same social pressures related to sin and redemptive sacrifice in the traditional code becomes an important means for the application of a new secular morality. Health is related to the way people behave and implies notions such as moral character and self-control. It is interesting to note that these ideas are similar to those in the beginning of the nineteenth century by the Temperance Movement (see Chapter 3).

Katz (ibid.) highlights some examples of the shift of attitude towards health, such as improvements in diet, exercise, hypertension detection, pharmacological control, and decreasing smoking (I further discuss anti-tobacco campaigns in Chapter 5). From this, a large segment of people came to believe that they could change their behaviour and benefit from a healthier 'lifestyle'. An interesting aspect of this morality is that this health movement can be seen as competing with religion in which '"good life" is extended life, not necessarily by religious morality but by a new belief in the new secular mythology about health and fitness' (ibid.: 301). In this sense, the traditional religious sources of eternal value have been shifted to a 'here and now' secular value system, while, at the same time, a relative mortality is won by the commitment to health and fitness.

Health discourses became the insignia of the new morality; it legitimises political intervention and individuals' behaviour, which is clearly illustrated in the discourses of addiction, often condemned as morally wrong and/or regarded as mental illness – a concept that is not value-free. Hence, Sedgwick (1992: 583) notes that 'the object of addiction has become, precisely, enjoyment of "the ability to choose freely, and freely to choose health"'.

From the establishment of this discourse, two aspects come into focus: the opposition between sin and disease, and the shift in people's discourses towards specific practices. Within the addiction field, 'risky practices' appear to involve a discursive shift from individual harm to social threat, for example the harm of smoking and the social threat produced by passive smoking. This health movement came to function as ethics of life; it prescribes behaviour, defines norms and constructs a moral justification for social surveillance, control and regulation (of the normal body).

It is relevant here to further analyse the understanding of ethics put forward here. Badiou (2001) points out that ethics, from the Greek, means: search for a good 'way of being', for a wise action. For the modern theorists, since Descartes, ethics has become close to morality; or for Kant as practical reason. Hegel introduces a distinction between ethics and morality, in which ethics is concerned with the immediate action and morality with reflexive action. Badiou (ibid.)

suggests that our contemporary moment is marked by a widespread 'return to Kant' (i.e. a concern with natural laws), in which there are representable imperative demands that are 'subjected neither to empirical considerations nor to the examination of situations' (ibid.: 8). These imperatives apply to cases of offence, of crime, of Evil, and they must be punished, and included therefore in legislation. In this way, ethics is conceived as an ability to discern evil and its judgement taken as a political judgement: 'good is what intervenes visibly against an Evil that is identifiable a priori' (ibid.: 8). This approach brings to the fore important questions around the universalism of constructions of evil and good, presupposing a universal understanding of man (taking up the term 'man' literally, I ask, which man is the universal man?).

In the contemporary scene, ethics are often related to the domain of human rights, thus assuming that there is a kind of natural right, such as the right to live, to avoid abusive treatment, and enjoy freedom. These rights are taken as self-evident and are the result of a wide consensus. In this way, Badiou (ibid.: 4) argues '"ethics" has become a matter of busying ourselves with these rights, of making sure that they are respected'. Criticising this use of ethics, Badiou (ibid.: 5) draws on Foucault's understanding of 'Man' as a 'constructed historical concept peculiar to a certain order of discourse, and not a timelessly self-evident principle capable of founding human rights or a universal ethics'. Badiou points out that this also applies 'by extension, for the self-evident, universal demarcation of evil, of what is incompatible with the human essence' (ibid.: 6).

'Ethics', rather, should be seen in its specific social and political location (including gender, sexuality, class, race, etc.) (Prado *et al.*, 2010), as well as the proper definition of 'rights', where 'human rights discourses see right as a property belonging to or conferred upon a person, rather than emerging between people' (Marks, 1996: 115), that is, from specific power relations.

Such critical perspectives on contemporary understandings of ethics are particularly relevant to health discourses, and more specifically to discourses of drugs and drug policies, as mainstream approaches to drugs claim a universal consensus of what is good and bad without taking into consideration the specifics of situations.

We have seen the (re)production of moral dichotomies within discourses of addiction such as, truth/false, natural/artificial, public/private. Here, the flexible notion of *pharmakon* was emphasised, and how the discursive opposition between free will and addiction operate, arguing for the need to socially and politically locate free will. Moreover, I identified moral and ethical values embedded in the discussion of drug use, and how discourses of health appear as an ethics of living. In the next chapters, I will focus on the social imaginary of drugs and drug users produced within these discursive foundations.

5 Drug use and the social imaginary

In this chapter, I analyse some of the effects of the polarised discursive positions of drugs and highlight some aspects of these social imaginary of the drug user and moral standpoints for the war on drugs. Discourses around drugs, seen here as (per)formative, produce specific positions, and are often polarised between that of victim or threat. The social imaginary is discussed not as an individual attribute, but as a subject position produced through power relations.

The drug user is often located as the 'other' in mainstream discourses, based on polarised positions of the victim and/or the plague. These discourses are strategically used according to specific aims. Medical discourses position the drug user as a victim of the disease addiction, therefore in need of medical care; this contrasts with other approaches that conceive the drug user as a threat, as such included in legislation, or as evil or as a source of bad influence for some religious discourses. In macro-politics, specific subjects and particular drugs are seen as a threat.

The war on drugs, drugs in war

Drawing on religious, medical and legal/state discourses on drugs, binaries and dichotomised discourses are identified, and these often provide a dual-only perspective on drugs. The malleable character of drugs (*pharmakon*, poison and remedy) is often obscured in mainstream discourse, where there is an attempt to extract only remedy for medicine (as if there are not non-wanted effects of medical drugs), and considering poison drugs that are not used by or for religious or medical prescription. As such, drugs are regulated and controlled, often producing political, medical and religious responses, and drug users condemned by religious authorities, criminalised and/or medicalised, constituting a specific form of biopolitics.

The main focus of this section is not on factual events of this 'war', but rather to discuss the moral grounds for the war and the political use of discourses of drugs in wars. It is important to note that the war on drugs is not only metaphorical, but rather concerns actual warfare officially or unofficially declared against producing groups at home and foreign countries (Chapter 3).

The 'other': victim and 'plague'

For this analysis, I focus on the production of the other, through the dynamics of the gaze. Foucault (1991) in *Discipline and Punish* emphasises the importance of situating culturally and historically techniques of punishment, whether they seize the body or are addressed to the 'soul'. Regarding disciplinary and surveillance mechanisms, it is important to point out that the 'examination combines the techniques of an observing hierarchy and those of a normalising judgement' (ibid.: 184). This is what constitutes a normalising gaze – a surveillance that enables it to qualify, classify and punish. Therefore, such practices establish over individuals a visibility in which one can differentiate and judge them.

These mechanisms of discipline (such as examination) are ritualised – they deploy force, establish 'truth' and produce subjectivity. It is important to note that the components of examination (rituals, methods, characters and their roles, plays of questions and answers, systems of marking and classification) also in their general and fluid forms, produce a domain of knowledge, a type of power. As Foucault (ibid.: 185) states, it is 'what makes possible knowledge that is transformed into political investment'. This examination process describes a technological scheme that became widespread in psychiatry, pedagogy and labour.

Drug discourses illustrate well these mechanisms of power, the production of specific bodies of knowledge and the establishment of specific 'truths'. Mechanisms of discipline can be seen in operation in drug classifications and examinations (e.g. drug tests). For the understanding of mechanisms of power and the dynamics of visibility-invisibility, it is relevant to look at Bentham's architectural figure of the 'Panopticon' (ibid.: 200):

> At the periphery, an annular building; at the centre, a tower, this tower is pierced with wide windows that open onto the inner side of the ring; the peripheral building is divided into cells, each of which extends the whole width of the building; they have two

> windows, one on the inside, corresponding to the windows of the tower; the other, on the outside, allows the light to cross the cell from one end to the other.

This model is seen as an ideal form of the mechanism of power, due to its polyvalent applications (schools, prisons, hospitals). For example, in the case of a prison, there is no danger of a plot or attempt of collective escape; in the hospital, no danger of contagion; in the school, it prevents copying, noise, at the work place, no danger of disorder.

From this model, the crowd is substituted by a collection of individuals, and it is the visibility provided by this building that guarantees order. 'From the point of view of the guardian, it is replaced by a multiplicity that can be numbered and supervised; from the point of view of the inmates, by a sequestered and observed solitude' (ibid.: 201). Hence, power is exerted here as visible and unverifiable. In terms of visibility, the inmate will always have the central tower from which he/she is surveyed, and it is unverifiable since he/she does not know whether he/she is being observed at any one moment; but one should be sure that one *may always be* looked at.

This model is particularly relevant here because it establishes the authoritative gaze, and it highlights how the gaze is not owned by one, but rather it is exerted by anybody. In the field of drugs, the gaze is particularly relevant, as, on the one hand, there are the authorities of drugs (stating who can take, what can take) and, on the other hand, because drugs are morally condemned – anyone has the moral space to intervene in other people's use of drugs.

Another metaphor relevant here is that of 'the plague-stricken town'. Developed by Foucault (ibid.), it points to specific mechanisms of power and control. The plague should be understood here as real and imaginary, a form of disorder that had its medical and political intervention. Under this disciplinary mechanism, there is the memory of 'contagions', plague, rebellions, crimes, vagabondage, desertions, disorder, meeting some of the ideas in circulation around drugs and drug users.

The 'plague' gave rise to disciplinary projects, including rituals of exclusion, and confinement. Here, the main power mechanisms are separation and its segmentations. Separation is marked, and segmentation is analysed and distributed (ibid.: 198). For separation, the notion of a pure community is evoked, and for segmentation a disciplined society. These two forms of exercising power control and regulate relationships by separating dangerous mixtures.

In mainstream discourses of drugs, drugs are seen as the plague (menace), as a disease invading the pure (social) body. While the drug user disrupts the social order, thus participating in the rituals of exclusion, they could also be seen as a source of bad influence themselves, or harming others (e.g. passive smoking).

Elaborating on key elements of mechanisms of power, Foucault suggests that, in a sense, all the authorities that exercise individual control function in accordance to a double mode; on the one hand, the binary divisions and branding (mad/sane, dangerous/harmless, normal/abnormal, victim/plague) and, on the other hand, the coercive assignment of differential distribution (who he/she is; where he/she must be; how he/she is to be characterised).

This dynamic is relevant in mainstream discourses of drugs, since drugs, most typically the illegal ones, are treated as plagues that should be extinguished (e.g. 'war on drugs'). On the other hand, the drug user, through the disease theory, is portrayed as a victim of the disease (which extends the victim position also in relation to the family, social class, body), and further, drug users carry the stigma of exclusion, as if capable of spreading the disease, for example by harming others, association with crime, and bad influence.

In the case of the 'plague-stricken town', this is understood as an exceptional situation, in which power is exercised against an extraordinary evil. The exercise of power here is visible and present. The 'plague' gave rise to an 'exceptional disciplinary model: perfect, but absolutely violent; to the disease that brought death' (ibid.: 207) (e.g. 'war on drugs'). By contrast, the 'panopticon' plays a role of amplification; although it arranges power and it is intended to make it more economic and more effective, it does so not for power itself, nor for the immediate salvation of a threatened society: 'its aim is to strengthen the social forces – to increase production, to develop economy, spread education, raise the level of public morality; to increase and multiply' (ibid.: 207–208), some examples are seen in relation to specific drug users.

From this account of power, some actions in relation to drugs can be conceptualised. On the one hand, as already pointed out, drugs can be seen as a plague that should be eliminated, the moral grounds for the 'war on drugs'. And, on the other hand, the mechanism of surveillance and discipline are found in discourses on drugs, more specifically in relation to moral binary hierarchies that these discourses produce: freedom/control, purity/impurity, truth and reality. Moreover discourses around drug users play both on the positions of the 'plague' and the 'victim', and are constantly surveilled. These dynamics bring forth a specific ethics.

Badiou (2001), in his essay on *Ethics*, discusses notions of evil, where 'evil' is commonly taken as universally identifiable (even when the universal contradicts 'public opinion'). From this a priori determination of evil, Badiou argues that this 'ethics prevents itself from thinking the singularity of situation' (ibid.: 14). For example, in the case of medicine, the doctor wins over to 'ethical ideology' all kinds of considerations in relation to 'the sick'. Badiou claims that this framework of 'ethics' should be rejected as it 'concedes nothing to the negative and victimary definitions of man' (ibid.: 16). Because of its abstract and statistical generality, it prevents us from thinking about the singularity of situations. Instead, Badiou asserts the need to contextualise ethics, as there are no ethics in general, but rather 'ethical processes by which we treat the possibilities of a situation' (ibid.: 16).

This assertion is important here for, in the case of drug use, a particular social imaginary of the drug user as a victim is put forward. And, crucially, as drug policies tend to be universal, they do not take the specifics of the situations into account, including the cultural, social values and political specificities; and laws are often introduced by force. Thus, the signifier 'health' can function as legitimisation for social intervention, as self-sufficient and self-evident, preventing a critical reading and alternative approaches in drug debates and drug policies.

Another key feature within this debate is the notion of 'difference'. The idea of the 'right to difference' is developed by Badiou (ibid.), pointing out that the ethics of human rights seem to define an identity and, in this way, the respect for the different applies to those who are 'reasonably consistent with this identity' (ibid.: 24). In this way, Badiou asks: 'the celebrated "other" is acceptable only if he is a good other (which is to say what, exactly if not the same as us?)' (ibid.: 24). Here, it is crucial to reflect on the drug user occupying the discursive space of the other.

The position of the 'other' of drugs and drug users will be utilised for the next analysis of the social imaginary of drugs as the enemy, and further social imaginary identifications of drug users.

The myth of drugs

As seen, macro-drug policies draw on a social imaginary of drugs as evil substances, bringing fear and panic. Here, there is a 'consensus' of who the enemy is, and it is discursively positioned as something that comes from outside, as if they are not part of the social context. As Bucher (1992) argues, there is a fantasy to eradicate psychoactive substances from social life, as if they are something occasional or superficial; an evil added from outside and not inherent to society. However, when drugs are treated in this way, they become a myth, carrying a series of non-spoken assumptions (ibid.), producing particular effects and legitimising social intervention, and as a myth they discursively increase the danger accorded to drugs and can function as 'scapegoat': an enemy jeopardising the harmony and balance of innocent populations.

The notion of scapegoat is used in models of group therapy, interpreted as emotional displacement, defence mechanism and as a group indication of projective identification (Taylor and Rey, 1953; Scheidlinger, 1982). The term 'scapegoat' comes from the Hebrew 'goat for Azazel', in which on the Day of the Atonement one or two goats were chosen and symbolically loaded with the sins of Jewish people. Later, one goat was sent over a cliff and the other burnt in the temple as a sacrifice (Scheidlinger, 1982). In Ancient Greece, the scapegoat was part of religious practice to protect communities from plagues, famine and other threats. Significantly, the person who was sacrificed as a scapegoat was called *pharmakos* (Szasz, 1975), symbolising the expulsion of the evil out of the body and out of the city (Derrida, 1997). Two aspects are highlighted here: the political function of scapegoats and the role of emotions, and the election of drugs as scapegoat.

The discursive polarisation produced in drug debates does not allow further analysis of drug use. Merely, it posits drugs as a sort of scapegoat, delimiting what is good and bad. It is important to bear in mind that because drugs (i.e. illegal drugs) are so imbued with negative connotations, emotions such as fear and panic play a fundamental role in these debates. As Dally (1996: 200) suggests:

> For individuals whose fears and fantasies have been stimulated by governments and doctors, the so-called 'drug crisis' and the 'War on Drugs' is largely a product of what Freud called primary process thinking, i.e. the thinking of fantasy and dreams, unfettered by fact (at least, by fact in context), unimpeded by logic, highly symbolic, and dominated by anomalies and mysteries.

We can hypothesise that, by naming the fear, there is a fantasy of managing the enemy of it, being easier to bear it, to master it. Psychoanalysis also reveals 'by naming what is going on, we cease to be ravished by it' (Frosh, 1995: 296).

Furthermore, it is relevant to consider the role of fear in this field. Ahmed (2003) suggests that fear is not conceived simply as an individual matter, but rather it has a social role – it aligns individuals with communities. The role of emotions is by 'sticking figures together (adherence), it creates the very effect of a collective (coherence)' (ibid.: 2). Emotions are thus economic; 'they circulate between signifiers in relationships of difference and displacement' (ibid.: 2). These signifiers, through their reiteration, create associations, and especially mobilising fear, re-open past histories. As Butler (1997: 140) suggests, 'one speaks a language that is never fully one's own, but that language only persists through repeated occasions of that invocation'. Although signifiers are not fixed, it is on the historical fixity of some signifiers (Ahmed, 2000) that we see how specific words are constantly reiterated, placing drugs and drug users in a specific discursive position.

These particular discourses on drugs are, in fact, often informed by moral and emotional accounts undermining critical analysis – they produce a sort of 'moral panic'. Ben-Yehuda (1994) points out that 'moral panic' relates to a condition or people identified as a threat to societal values. These are represented in stereotypical ways by mass media and diagnoses and solutions delivered by experts, elements indicative of the terrain of drug debates.

Political interventions and drug policies readily draw on this social imaginary of drugs as 'plague'. Although the reasoning for this war was never completely specified (Lenson, 1995), the war on drugs is reactivated according to political circumstances (Goldberg, 1999). In this context, these take the forms of a fight against an evil and the defence of good such that, in this context, actions can be taken that, in a different situation, would meet strong resistance, such as changes in priorities and dismissal of rational arguments. Indeed, this kind of war can also work to divert public opinion from other political matters. As Hugh-Jones (1995: 48) puts it, 'this reified emphasis on substances rather than in on people results in a shift in attention away from the social forces that lie behind the consumption'. Two main aspects are highlighted here: how discourses of the 'war on drugs' function in politics, and the moral and ethical standpoints evoked within these mainstream discourses on drugs.

Law

Within this hyper moral-emotional arena of debates on drugs, the location and formation of the 'plague' is identified, as well as those who participate in this: drug users and drug dealers. From the perspective of the law, everyone who infringes the law is a criminal, including the illegal drug user.

The legislation of drugs constitutes a conundrum, since definitions of drugs are ambiguous and contradictory, 'in terms of function and effects of drugs, the law is arbitrary' (Loose, 2002a: 272), particularly considering mood-changing medical drugs and illegal drugs. It is important to highlight that the Designer Drugs Act (USA) (1971) states that *every psychofarmaco non authorised* previously is under the same regimen of prohibition as the illegal ones. Escohotado (1998: 221, vol. 3) argues that this is, 'a revolutionary precept but, instead of specifying substances, it inaugurates the principle in which everything that is not authorised is forbidden'. Some considerations on the enactment of laws are relevant here. Oenen (2000a) points out that, 'law is something established through force, it always remains marked and haunted by its foundational trauma. If the wound of this trauma is reopened, latent constitutional forces are awakened and actualised, usually destabilising a presently existing interpretive consensus'.

One of the effects of this enforcement is that it makes legislations appear abstract, not allowing for analysis of its social meanings. Laws appear to be self-contained, self-fulfilled, and in a sense self-authorising and self-validating. Moreover, Oenen (2000b) highlights that the tensions in the rule of law or between law and reality cannot be eliminated, but rather strategies are developed to cope with these tensions (e.g. *gedogen* – deliberate lax enforcement of the law).

Law most commonly intervenes in areas that are seen as morally wrong, such as in the realms of drugs and sex. It is relevant to examine the effect of law in relation to pleasure, and particularly body pleasures. Foucault (1978) points out how interventions worked in relation to sex, telling the truth of sex as power (knowledge) and the rituals of confession, which were stimulated and required. Foucault (1978/1976) highlights rituals of confession used in religious, medical, in the family and other contexts, and that we have in fact become a confessing society.

Klein (1995), elaborating on Foucault's *History of Sexuality*, gives an account of two types of law utilised to control pleasure: the interdictions related, for example, to the laws against adultery in the Middle Ages, and for initiation there were rules and regulations against masturbation predominant in the nineteenth century, applied by doctors, priests, families and pedagogues. Klein points out that making masturbation a vice did not decrease the practice, but rather it enlarged the idea of what it is. Juxtaposing this to drugs, one of the effects of the intervention of law was the enlargement of the power of the enemy, as seen in the case of the use of drugs before and after prohibition.

The enemy

Here, I further elaborate on the political function of drugs as enemy and how *pharmakon* operates for the election of scapegoat. By producing and identifying the enemy, the power and location of the enemy is enlarged, mobilising responses of fear and anxiety, and the enemy is placed in the position of the 'other'. Indeed, Coomber (1998: xii in South, 1999: 11) highlights:

> The existing drug control policies may have developed from a drug-centric foundation of exaggeration and falsity, interrelated with notions of 'otherness' (xenophobia/racism) and misplaced (and essentially contradictory) moralities as well as international and national politics, among other biases, that until these influences have been acknowledged and neutralised, rational debate on drugs and drug use controls will remain difficult.

This feature of 'otherness' of drugs found in mainstream discourses does not apply of course to drugs utilised in medical or religious contexts, and in this sense, Goldberg (1999) questions if drugs came to replace the devil in secularised societies.

The production and identification of the enemy function in various ways, and this can unite forces against a common enemy. Goldberg points out that 'if drugs are defined as absolutely bad, totally lacking ameliorating qualities, we can unite with others in unreserved loathing without transgressing socially acceptable boundaries' (Goldberg, 1999). Dally (1996) highlights how this war is based on misinformation and is not in fact concerned with individuals and drugs. Here, the signifier 'health' is utilised as self-evident and self-sufficient, and many times decontextualised, discursively legitimising the war on drugs. In this sense, Ruggiero (1999: 133) argues that:

> Drug prohibition promotes a political use of the criminal justice system, which is apparent in these propaganda symbols. These symbols are aimed at the mobilisation of consensus, and are less effective in preventing harmful behaviour than in satisfying 'expressions of disapproval' among sectors of society.

Turning to the election of the enemy, it seems that the character of *pharmakon* of not having a stable form (Derrida, 1997) fits into this space. Thus, on the one hand, it can cause fear for its polyvalent qualities, and, on the other hand, it can be used strategically in discourse. *Pharmakon* located in the position of the 'other' (i.e. different from 'us') functions as a perfect enemy. Chomsky (1991: 114) highlights some aspects of the choice of the war on drugs: the menace should be portrayed as grave, targets should be weak enough not to be costly, and 'the wrong colour also helps. The menace should be situated in the Third World, whether abroad or in the inner city at home'. Other authors also highlight qualities for the 'suitable enemy'. South (1999: 9), drawing on Christie (1986: 42–43) outlines some elements:

> (1) major problems will not be defined in ways that threaten centrally-positioned and powerful groups in society. The enemy must not be defined in such a way that strong groupings line up behind him and object to the definition of the problem as a problem; (2) a good enemy ought to be seen as dangerous, often inhuman; (3) the enemy is so strong that extraordinary powers are granted; (4) good enemies are those that never die . . . 'The enemy is almost exterminated' the war-bulletins claim, 'just give us some more time and resources and the job will be done'. Wars fought by professional experts against unclear and vaguely defined targets are particularly suitable. In such cases the enemy can be defined so that suitable targets can be included or excluded according to needs; (5) the greater an evil, the more such an enemy can unite and dissolve other conflicts within any society.

These elements correspond well to the social imaginary of drugs. Moreover, Christie (ibid.) presents three major features in relation to drugs as the perfect enemies:

> (1) it is unclear what should be defined as narcotics. The enemy can be changed according to needs [meeting the here the notion of *pharmakon*]; (2) as with drugs, so with users. Actions are directed towards those most suitable [e.g. marginalised people]; (3) as with users, so too with the producers [and distributors], attention is directed toward the most 'suitable' [e.g. not applied to legal drugs].

These arguments draw on a particular social imaginary of drugs, that of the 'enemy'. Here, drugs symbolise the imagined 'other' that threatens the individual and the nation. Further, the idea of the 'enemy out there', makes explicit the decontextualisation of drugs, as if *pharmakon* is not part of social and cultural practices, a plague coming from outside. 'Out there' is significant for a social imaginary of drugs as foreign, non-Western, 'as the immigrants coming to the industrialised world from all over the globe' (Goldberg, 1999: 5). This association can provoke further implications, for example by linking to specific minority groups (e.g. African Americans in the US, Chinese in the UK) (Murji, 1999) (see Chapter 3). Further, coming from afar increases fear, 'fear of the unknown' (Goldberg, 1999: 5), risking (re)producing particular racist and xenophobic discourses.

Social imaginary of drug users

As pointed out before, images of the victim and threat/plague inform imaginaries of the drug user. We can summarise this as follows: victim of the drug habit, of bad influences, of neurological dysfunctions, and threat by being prejudicial to others by directly damaging the health of others (e.g. cigarette smoking), bad influence, for drug related crimes or participating in the illegal market of drugs (consuming or dealing).

Before we continue, as I expressed before, in no sense do I deny specific individual and social problems regarding drugs. However, it is still the case that discourses on drugs produce specific effects (exaggerations, moral panics), particularly impacting to the individual who uses drugs.

The body is politically invested in relation to drug use, regarded as the governments' obligation to ensure a clean and productive body. Hence, the body here is a political force, as Foucault (1991: 25–26) points out: 'the body is also directly involved in a political field; power relations have an immediate hold upon it; they invest it, mark it, train it, torture it, force it to carry out tasks, to perform ceremonies, to emit signs'. This investment is related to the economic use, and labour power, 'the body becomes a useful force only if it is both a productive body and a subjected body' (ibid.: 25–26). The biopolitics of drugs can be seen at its full extent.

As seen, drug users are typically viewed as sinners, criminals or mentally ill (Mountian, 2006), as also noted by Shapiro (1999: 18): 'mad, bad or sad', and Young (1971): immoral, without norms or sick. However, other current forms of drug use have been challenging this image, such as the use of ecstasy by the youth, which I discuss in Chapter 6. These categories shift across discourse, operating strategically according to the context. Hence, these categories should not be taken as the only possible imaginaries of drug users, yet these illustrate key aspects of discourses of drug users, by combining key institutional elements in drug discourses: medical, legal and religious.

The division proposed in the chapter follows this logic. However, these discourses appear intertwined in everyday language. The analysis does not focus on individuals, but rather on the discursive structures evoked by these accounts. The following extracts are primarily based on the interviews conducted in Brazil and in England from previous research (Mountian, 1999, 2004a). Further, I do not claim that all Western countries approach drugs in the same way, as these should be seen in specific social and political contexts, considering gender, sexuality, class, race, age and disability. Nonetheless, the examples pointed out here work as indicative of current social imaginaries of drug users.

Madness – medical discourses

The social imaginary of 'madness' is central in discourses on drug use, as drug addiction is classified as a mental illness. However, these medical discourses are not neutral, but rather they are socially and politically specific, and often carry negative connotations in lay discourses.

In previous research (Mountian, 2004a), a range of examples were highlighted by drug users (or ex-users) regarding the association between drug use and madness, as well as of medical understandings of drugs. Summarising, these were: social prejudice against drug users, image of the drug user as analogous to the image of the mad person, fear of madness by taking drugs, fear of addiction by using drugs, misinformation, fear of 'psychotic crisis', understandings of addiction as a disease in terms of chemical dependency, the result of the effects of the drugs in the brain, and medical explanations for explaining the disease including psychological profiles such as lies, dissimulation, non acceptance of rules, emotional difficulties. In fact, Singleton (2010), in research conducted with 2,945 people in the UK, pointed out that the public hold more negative attitudes and tolerance towards drug users than to those with mental health issues, as they are seen as blameworthy for their use, while drug use is generally seen as an illness of a chronic condition. Some examples are seen here:

D: I think that there is prejudice, who doesn't use sees the person who uses as a mad person, or a person lacking something that they are looking for.

G: A chemical dependent is an ill person, a disease that we have.

G: The characteristic of chemical dependent is the lie, the dissimulation, difficulty to accept rules.

These extracts meet Young's (1971: 73) discussion on the relationship between doctors and drug users in which 'these individuals perceive themselves as having primarily the therapeutic role of assimilating "the poor", "the maladjusted", "the immature personality", "the undersocialised", "the sick", "the adolescent gone-wrong", and experts are the only ones who can understand them.' The role of this position has been discussed in Chapter 4.

Free will – victim – moral discourses

Here, I discuss a social imaginary of the 'victim' of drug users and on understandings of addiction, drawing on the notions of free will and control, which appear in opposition to dependency. Dependency is often discursively positioned as opposed to strength, an undesirable quality, a weakness, a feminised feature (see Chapter 6).

Before we proceed, the debate on stigma is relevant here. Stigma derives from *stigmata* and refers to a mark on the body, identifying the person permanently with his/her disgrace. For the ancient Greeks, this would be inflicted as the punishment for treason, or running away from a master, marking the person as spoiled, not the deed, the equivalent to Goffman's (1963) modern metaphor for 'spoiled identity' (Warner, 1999).

It is relevant to highlight some effects of dynamics of stigma for the subject, particularly on the 'acceptance' of this discursive position by the drug user and the social consequences of the stigma, when they accept this position – 'their kingdom is not from this world' (Xiberras, 1989: 202). Reflecting on the identification of the drug user as addict or ex-user, discursive possibilities of identification are limited, as they are reduced only to the relationship with the drug. Identification then circulates around this specific signifier, thus not allowing other forms of identification of the subject: one is always a user, or an ex-user.

Furthermore, it is possible to reflect on how this stigma may also contribute to certain forms of intoxication and what the effects of this imaginary are. Indeed, Xiberras (1989) argues that the stigmatisation of drug users can lead them to increase their practices of intoxication. In the same direction, Dally (1996: 201) points out that addicts (whether patients or not) have low self-esteem, and this is also related to the way they are viewed in society and by medical institutions: 'They still feel they have to play the part of the degraded, dying creatures that society wants them to be'. In fact, clinical studies have focused on the guilt and low self-esteem of the user (Olievenstein *et al.*, 1989). Stigmatisation of drug users has been highlighted in research in the UK, pointing out problems associated to this position, such as exclusion, difficulties of recovery and obtaining jobs (Lloyd, 2010).

From interviews conducted in previous research (Mountian, 1999, 2004a) a number of discourses around control and power emerged, particularly emphasising the position of the loser, weak, ill, coward, lacking strength, infantilised, inconsiderate, immature and decadent, and on apathy and death, these meet other studies (e.g. Young, 1971, on the drug user as childish, weak and seductive). Some examples are:

T: I didn't feel a proper person.
L: I'm an ugly sod.
L: They think I'm useless.
B: A person who doesn't have prejudice, sees as a poor thing, weak, this is how I see it today, not a poor thing, but a weak, an ill person. I see even as a coward. I can say that I was a coward, I feel that I was a coward like, for everything I've done, when I was using drug, to get drug and after I was using drug and the use itself of drug.
G: All chemical dependents are like this, childish, weak and seductive.
J: It is associated with a kind of decadence, a kind of uselessness . . . This imaginary relies on this, on a supposed apathy.

These extracts point to aspects of the social imaginary of drug users as weak, apathetic, cowardly, useless, and lacking strength occupying a specific social position. It is relevant to highlight how the idea of uselessness and dependency relate to productivity. Some interviews (Mountian, 1999, 2004a) point out that, for productivity, there is an idea of being in control that does not match with the notions of uncontrollability of drug use, while some also point out that some drugs function better for specific types of work.

These images on weakness contrast to other uses of drugs, for example on the images of cigarettes and pipes, which are seen as the 'emblem of stability and strength, and the cigarette of insecurity and weakness' (Penn, 1901 in Walton, 2000: 83). Similarly, Klein (1995: 32) observes:

> Smoking cigarettes engenders the gauze pleasure of ephemera . . . Conversely, the pipe accompanies the labour of the negative, dreams of a more heroic sort, like the grave undertaking of pure poetry . . . Pipes are adult, serious, grave, while cigarettes are childish, irresponsible, flimsy veils.

Moreover, death plays an important role in drug discourses. The analysis of the drug policy 'no to drugs, yes to life' brings some insights. The 'no to drugs, yes to life' policy targets the private sphere, a policy addressed to individuals' behaviour, while the 'war on drugs' is a national and international policy. In the mottos 'just say no' or 'no to drugs, yes to life', there is at first a protective or paternalistic approach in which 'just say no' (one should consider that it is important to have more information in order to say no) somehow presupposes a (evil) person offering drugs to innocent ones.

The idea of 'no to drugs, yes to life' also carries a message that yes to drugs would equate to yes to death. In this sense, it is possible to point out that those who use drugs does not necessarily mean yes to death. Rather, meanings of drug use should be seen individually, and socially contextualised. Drugs can also be used as form of celebration of life (e.g. alcohol on birthdays), or as a form of coping with life. Here, it is possible to juxtapose this idea with the phenomenon of self-harm. Through its ambivalent character, it can be related to surviving rather than suicide (Spandler and Bastleer, 2000).

Crime – legal discourses

Illegality of drugs is a key aspect in drug debates, from the 'war on drugs' to the glamour and power of drug taking (I discuss this in later sections). The need to consider effects of stigmatisation of the drug user as a criminal has been discussed in previous research (Hunt and Stevens, 2004; Radcliffe and Stevens, 2008). Here, I highlight discourses on drug users as criminals or immoral people and the drug user seen as a menace to the community. From the interviews, some examples are:

Z: The guy who uses drugs turns into an E.T., an outlaw.

J: As a user of marijuana, an aspect that I feel uncomfortable with is in relation to a condition of delinquency somehow, or of legal contrariety, and this is the first thing that annoys me, because actually I don't feel at all an offender. Anyway, of any aspect from one of these that constitutes a citizen.

T: I always felt like a second class citizen inside

W: I was smoking too much marijuana, then no, I was seeing myself as a little delinquent (*maloqueirinha*), you are a rubbish, girl (*lixo mina*), you are a zero on the left, you are useless, I was seeing myself like this, a little addict (*viciadinha*).

S: As weak people, lost, as losers, as people that one cannot trust, as people capable of hideous acts, of evil acts, as perverse people, promiscuous, as people . . . I think that there is a demonisation of the user of drugs in general, in society.

These examples highlight the discursive position of delinquency, of not being a citizen, non-productivity and dangerousness. Regarding citizenship, these examples meet the underlying assumptions within discourses on the pathology of addiction, implying lack of rationally and self-control, which are qualities expected for moral agency and citizenship (Keane *et al.*, 2011).

Regarding crime, the position of being an outlaw was expressed, but also resisted (see also Radcliffe and Stevens, 2008). The element of 'otherness' figures profoundly within drug use. In these examples and in previous research (Mountian, 2004a), interviewees pointed out that drug users (and drug dealers) are seen as threats, prevailing an image of the drug user as a criminal, where drugs and crime were often linked: delinquency, criminality, evilness, promiscuity, immorality, liars, also meeting aspects of other studies that highlight drug users as dangerous, deceitful, unreliable (Lloyd, 2010). It is important to emphasise that I do not deny the existence of drug-related crimes, but in order to enlarge the discussion on drug use, I point out the extension of these imaginary formations and how they inform governmental practices and public opinion. I emphasise here the position of the 'other' in discourse. As Becker (1963: 9) points out, deviance is not an individual quality, but rather 'the deviant is one to whom the label has successfully been applied; deviant behaviour is behaviour that people so label'.

In relation to criminality, class plays an important role, where social imaginary of drug taking varies according to class, and working classes are discursively positioned as more prompted to criminality, naturalising crime, drug use and the connection between both, as illustrated in Chapter 3.

Hence, it is relevant to highlight that the popular use of the term 'junkie', which was coined from the New York City rubbish collectors in 1920, and it was conferred upon heroin users who sold scrap metal collected from industrial dumps to support their habit, associated then with rubbish and criminality, contrasting to morphine users for medical illness. The use of the term 'junk' as drug (rather than the metal) and 'junkies' for drug users was after William Burroughs' publication *Junkie* in 1940 (Radcliffe and Stevens, 2008). Radcliffe and Stevens point out that this is still present, and this has negative effects on the subject, particularly heroin users. As anti-drug campaigns do not consider the possibility of controlled use of heroin, associating with this image of junkies, also in drug treatment, this can work as preventing people from seeking help, as for many users treatment and segregation in pharmacies are seen as stigmatising and humiliating.

Immorality (passive smoking)

For the analysis of discourses on the immorality of drug users, I focus on the analysis of anti-tobacco campaigns and mainstream discourses on smokers. For this analysis, I focus on how the signifier 'health' is used in discourse and its effects, such as the production of a moral standpoint for legitimisation for social intervention, emphasising moral components intrinsic to these campaigns. Again, I do not deny that cigarettes may cause harm for the individual and those around them, but I focus on the moral context that these campaigns are embedded in, and how these political actions represent and produce some known divisions.

Currently, anti-tobacco campaigns seem to be winning many battles against smokers. Here, there is a strong element of separatism, in which strategic actions such as excluding smokers from public spaces are taking place. The main argument against cigarette smoking is that of causing harm to others, specifically passive smoking. Some researchers, however, have argued that the level of smoking that can be harmful to others is not yet defined, 'the hypothesis that extremely low and intermittent exposure to ETS poses a significant public health threat is yet to be demonstrated' (Gostin, 1997: 348).

Regarding the separation between smokers and non-smokers, some employers have taken a more radical approach – they have banned smoking at work, in the car, or at home in some countries (ibid.). I am not going to comment further on this, but we could question the intervention within the private sphere.

Focusing on smoking, it is relevant to point out that banning smoking from public buildings provoked a series of effects and reactions. For example, not providing indoor spaces for smokers can be seen as hazardous for their health, particularly in cold weathers. Further, it is known that a large number of pubs closed after the ban on smoking in England. The reasons for the closure are not clear yet (e.g. economic crisis), however after the ban a number of customers are opting to stay in uncontrolled environments free to drink and smoke, such as their home, bringing about a change in the tradition of pubs in England with the resultant effect on the economy.

Hence, smoking nowadays has been propagated as a particularly immoral act (Tracy and Acker, 2004), and somehow it becomes implicit that smokers 'deserve' their place (in the rain), where the separatist approach to cigarette smoking is reiterated. In this sense, it is interesting to note the example of a health quiz in a Manchester student magazine entitled, 'Are you a slob?' (*Pulp Magazine*, 2002), in which the active smoker is portrayed as harmful for the health of others (question 2) 'I don't smoke and I'm not usually surrounded by people who do'. It is interesting to note that, in the results, for 'too healthy', the conclusion is, 'Health Freak – there is a danger you are too healthy', again calling for a specific regulation of behaviour, perhaps the risk of becoming an 'addict to health styles' (gym addiction, organic food addiction, water drinking addiction).

Following a series of actions against smoking, tobacco packaging warning messages have been implemented in a number of countries, emphasising similar messages. These labels cover the back of the cigarette pack. The Food and Drug Administration (FDA) (2011) will require graphic warning labels that cover half a package's front and rear and the top 20 per cent of all cigarette advertisements. The *Los Angeles Times* (2010) says that:

> The labels will feature either drawings or photos illustrating graphically the dangers associated with smoking and will be accompanied by text stating that smoking is addictive or that it kills. The pictures feature such things as a diseased lung, a corpse and a man smoking a cigarette through a tracheotomy tube. They are not quite as grim as some used in other countries, but regulators hope they will be sufficiently frightening to keep young people from beginning to smoke and to strengthen the will of those who are attempting to quit.
>
> (Maugh, 2010)

These cigarette warnings are an example of drug policies, drawing on the 1950s style of fright in order to avoid smoking. It is clear that some of these images are very hard to bear (dying people, operations, rotten teeth, etc.). I cannot of course evaluate here the effectiveness of such campaigns, but perhaps exposing people who smoke to these images should be questioned. It seems that, because of the place that smokers came to occupy in society (scourge, immoral), they deserve to be exposed to these images, to smoke outside of buildings, to be questioned for health treatment, etc. – a punishment for their misdeed.

The analysis of a number of cigarette warnings in diverse countries (e.g. UK, US, Brazil) shows that they follow similar messages. I have separated these warnings into five groups: (1) related to death, for example 'smokers die younger', 'smoking can cause a painful and slow death' ('death' plays a crucial role in discourses of drugs); (2) warnings related to pregnancy, and passive smoking (harm to children); (3) physical harm (smoking can cause cancer and other examples such as, heart attack, sexual impotence, etc.); (4) messages concerning smoking prevention or cessation ('choose freedom, we'll help you'); and (5) the final group discloses the contents of the tobacco (although I am not sure if the public is aware of what this means).

The images vary from country to country; some are more shocking than others, dying people, dead babies, opened chests, nervous system exposed. In reaction to this, some smokers tend to cover the slogans with a piece of paper or using decorative cigarette cases. For example, in England, stickers were produced with sayings such as, 'You could get hit by a bus tomorrow' or 'Smoking makes you look hard'. Gostin (1997: 348) points out that these campaigns bring an image of smokers as immoral and inconsiderate, particularly for harming the health of children. Children 'are the so-called innocent victims of tobacco smoke, as if those who do smoke are morally blameworthy'. In this sense, smoking in front of a child would be regarded as a strongly immoral act. Moreover, there is a gender aspect in relation to drug policies, in which custody plays an important role in relation to the drug-using mother. I further elaborate on this in Chapter 7.

In the interviews, there is some resistance to these anti-smoking policies:

Z: I think that there is a surveillance with cigarettes, people look at you strangely . . . when they prohibited cigarette but there wasn't control, people started coughing in your ears . . . Talking to a friend on the Internet, he started saying that I have a problem, that I am going to die of cancer, because cigarette is the first, second and third cause of death in the US, then, I should stop at that moment. Then I tried to tell him, in my way, look, this fits into my life, helps with my anxiety, helps me to wake up in the morning, helps me to concentrate in my thoughts, I don't have lung problems now, and I don't see meaning in stopping . . . I don't think I am doing anything wrong.

Z: I think there is very little respect accorded the smoker . . . as if smoking is a meaningless act, there is a violence from those people

> who say: 'I wish smokers would die'. Nobody understands that the cigarette is important, when I am desperate, very anxious, nobody understands that cigarettes are important, and I think that this is lack of respect . . . And I think it is incredible how these people announce all the statistics from the WHO [World Health Organization], everything they read in the magazines.

These extracts, while pointing to a resistance of this discursive location, highlight the current image of immorality attached to smoking, and claiming to consider the meaning of cigarette smoking for the subject. Contemporary discourses on smoking meet some same imaginaries of illegal drug use, immorality, threat to children, death. As Klein (1995: 182) notes, a 'form of obscenity', and this obscenity is taken as a public health issue. 'Of course, censors always claim that they work on behalf of the moral and physical well-being of the body politic, which proscribed symbolic behaviour' (ibid.: 182). Hence, with this anti-tobacco campaign, this moral foundation has been revitalised, and consequently this provides scope for extra surveillance, separation, stigmatisation and social pressure for smokers to quit smoking.

This is one example of the changing attitudes based on the anti-tobacco campaign, which illustrates the moral basis of debates in the drug area. Also, it is important to stress how these campaigns produce scope for this kind of public reaction, in which the citizen becomes both the representative and the supervisor of health.

Within this analysis, the signifier 'health' emerges as clearly equated to moral and ruled life, evoking, on the one hand, the idea of health and morality prevalent in the nineteenth and twentieth centuries, and, on the other hand, these specific discourses on morality and health illustrate mechanisms of power and control (Foucault, 1991). Beyond discourses on physical harm by smoking, it has highlighted the moral ground drawn by and generated in these campaigns, and as such alternative approaches are often not considered (e.g. smoking areas in restaurants, clubs, coffee shops, smoking in bus queues, etc.).

Prohibition, transgression, fetish and glamour

Although there is no space to discuss further relations between prohibition and drug use here, I cite some aspects that I believe are important to consider. In any case, undoubtedly after prohibition the relationship with drugs suffered a radical change.

Some studies (O'Bryan, 1989; South, 1999) point out how prohibition and transgression can be seen, in some contexts, as part of a certain glamour and curiosity attached to drugs, and how transgression can also be seen related to power. I highlight here some aspects that are relevant for further discussion (Mountian, 2004a), the analysis of the relationship between the subject and the object-drug through the notion of fetish (Freud, 1977; Marx, 1990; Lacan, 1995; McClintock, 1995), particularly on the investment in the object, the enchantment, and the fixation (Gurfinkel, 1996); how secrecy is an important aspect within this context (Sedgwick, 1991; Foucault, 1998); and aspects regarding the *joiussance* of repetition (Lacan, 1994) of drug use.

Because of this social imaginary, as previously highlighted, a moral ground is identified and reinstated, producing specific public reactions and reiterating particular social imaginaries. Lack of information about illegal drugs is an important aspect that has further implications for the individuals as the consequences of the war on drugs, such as crime, violence, and moral panics associated as highlighted. Next, I examine these aspects of the social imaginary of drug users in relation to gender.

6 Gender in the social imaginary of drugs

In previous chapters, elements of the social imaginary of drug users were identified, in which the position of the 'other' was seen and elaborated according to the discursive positions of 'victim' and 'plague'. This chapter highlights how gender intersects with these positions, focusing on images around women, and elaborate on discursive aspects of 'dependency', 'weakness', 'vulnerability' 'uncontrollability,' 'madness' and 'immorality'. This intersection reproduces specific social imaginaries of female drug users and informs policies (which are largely male-oriented) around and about drugs. My focus here is on both discourses of women who use drugs, and on the gendering of some key features of the social imaginary of drug users.

Mainstream discourses of the drug user (re)produce the division between 'us' and 'them', positing the drug user as the 'other' in discourse. Elaborating on the position of the 'other' in discourse, it is relevant to highlight that 'women' are often portrayed and constituted as the 'other' in social and psychological spaces (Nieves, 1994; Burman, 2000). In this sense, it important to interrogate how the otherness of female drug users operates and to map the discursive positions that women who use drugs occupy. For this analysis, it is crucial to consider sexuality, race, age, class, and other social hierarchical structures. The objective of the focus on gender is to unravel the imaginary of the 'other' as (culturally) feminine (i.e. beyond biological determinations), as lacking, and the relationship with drug use.

It is important to reiterate that the discursive categories presented in this chapter (as in previous ones) are not taken as separate, for often they are intertwined with other discourses, and there is no intention to limit the social imaginary only to these discursive categories. Crucially, the social imaginary aspects explored in this chapter concern dominant Western discourses on drugs and gender, which also vary according to specific social and political contexts of Western countries (considering race, class, age, sexuality).

This chapter is organised in four main sections: the first draws on the position of the victim, drawing on discourses of 'weakness', 'dependency', 'control' and 'madness'. From this, I highlight the symbolic position of women in relation to nation. In the third section, 'threat', I elaborate on the dynamics of visibility and invisibility in relation to women and drug use, and finally, I highlight antagonistic aspects of the imaginary of women and drugs in relation to power. Key aspects of this imaginary of women and drugs in relation to drug policies are developed in Chapter 7.

The 'other'

The notion of the 'other' drawn upon here is mainly based on Foucauldian (see Chapter 5), gender studies approaches (feminist research and queer studies), and on aspects of the Lacanian psychoanalytic notion of the other. Psychoanalysis reveals some useful aspects for this analysis. As J. Rose (1994: 43) highlights, 'the unconscious constantly reveals the "failure" of identity. Because there is no continuity of psychic life, so there is no stability of sexual identity, no position for women (or for men) which is ever simply achieved.' However, failure for psychoanalysis is not an individual inadaptation or deviance. Rather, ' "failure" is something endlessly repeated and relived moment by moment throughout our individual histories' (ibid.).

The other is a key concept in Lacanian psychoanalysis, the big Other (*Autre*) is differentiated from the other (*autre*). The little other is related to dual relations, developed through the mirror stage, it incorporates the illusion of completeness of the subject, related to identification and relaton with the other. It corresponds to the imaginary order, the image, the other subject. The big Other, in this sense, refers to the symbolic order, to alterity, to language (law) that which proceeds the subject, it transcends it, being feared and admired. The other refers to the other subject, the Other to a position occupied by the subject. These dimensions are connected and function in relation to the real (which is unattainable, *Das Ding*).

The acknowledgment of the other as unitary is highlighted by Neill (2011) in order to avoid the recognition of the other as the different to me, a regime of differences. *Das Ding* does not belong to anybody, but it is experienced in the relation with the subject.

The big Other is taken here as a symbolic position, that which cannot be reached (André, 1991). The first Other is the mother. Lack and desire are articulated in Lacanian theory, in which it is the lack that causes desire. The lack in the symbolic is the lack in the Other, related then to the desire of the Other.

The Other refers to the symbolic network 'regulated according to language-like rules; and as a psychical structure, representative of this social Other, internalised in the form of the unconscious' (Grosz, 1990: 117). This conception of the Other is related to austerity and authority, to being unreachable, mysterious and also frightening.

Frosh (1995) highlights how this bears on the position of 'woman' in Lacanian theory. Woman is to be understood as a (non) symbolic location (function):

> Lacan claims that the essentially patriarchal organisation of culture, or properly speaking the phallic structuring of language, means that woman takes up her place as the Other, as something which stands outside the Symbolic as its negative, giving it its presence through her exclusion.
>
> (ibid.: 291)

Outside language means here outside power. However, it is relevant to point out from Saussure's linguistics that the signifier is not isolated but dependent on the entire system of signifiers. So in this sense, as Frosh (ibid.: 293) puts it, 'not only historically, in terms of her reproductive function, but also continually, in terms of her impact on the whole order of things – symbolic as well as imaginary – the woman makes the masculine exist'.

There is a longstanding debate on psychoanalysis in feminist research, in which psychoanalysis has been criticised and studied by feminist scholars (Cixous, 1976; Kristeva, 1982; Irigaray, 1989; Butler, 1999; Moi, 2010). It expresses tensions as well as insights among them, since psychoanalysis theorises understandings of gender and sex (J. Rose, 1994). In this way, for example, feminist psychoanalysts point out that patriarchy is seen as working on all levels (conscious and unconscious). As Stacey (1993: 57) notes, 'feminist work on the psychic dimensions of patriarchy has explored ways in which the broader structures of society operate within kinship relations in the formation of individuals identities'.

I will utilise some notions of psychoanalysis in order to reveal imaginary positions of women in discourse, thus the notions of the Other/other from the psychoanalysis of Lacan and the Foucauldian 'other' are explored here.

Victim

In this section, I focus on the social imaginary of the 'victim' of drug users and the relation with gender. Gendering the 'victim' position brings up two aspects: the idea of women as primary victims of drugs and the understanding of 'victim' as feminised.

The imaginary of 'victim' associated with drug users, as discussed in Chapter 5, is seen in a number of discourses, such as the user as victim of drugs, the user as victim of neurological, genetic or psychological dysfunctions, victim of 'addiction disease', etc. The victim position in discourse, as has been seen, produces specific effects, it can function displacing the responsibility of the user, it gives scope for social control, and at the same time paradoxically, it can also work to resist ideas such as the natural 'spoiled personality' of the user. Here, I do not ignore that some people are or see themselves as victims, however the focus is on the discursive effects of this position. In the case of women who use drugs, as Ettorre (1989: 105) argues, by positing female drug users as helpless victims, 'the subordination of women remains undisputed'.

Within discourses of the victim, control plays a key discursive role, implying that the drug user is 'out of control', and control is often equated with power and strength. In the analysis of discourses on uncontrollability and women and drugs, a range of discourses are highlighted, such as women being weaker than men in relation to drugs (physical strength), or weaker in their personality (more prone to drug addiction and to madness). Further, uncontrollability is often associated with (their) sexuality as I will now go on to analyse.

Madness

For medicine and psychiatry, addiction is a mental illness (e.g. DSM and ICD), related to biological and/or psychological (mal)functions. This model focusing on the individual does not consider social contexts and social structural positioning; it becomes a matter of the individual and the pathology. Engendering madness, I highlight how madness is often feminised, and how the term 'madness' operates in relation to women.

Feminist researchers point out that madness associated to women produces a range of effects, symbolically (positioning them as 'other') and materially (e.g. on the prescription of antidepressants, see Chapter 3), and often madness is associated with their sexuality. Finally, as Warner (1996) points out, madness functions as a signifier that locates women outside, as ill ('somehow second rate'), the second-sex. Furthermore, these discourses produce an understanding of madness as feminised, 'as fearful, as individual, as invariably feminine, as sickness' (Ussher, 1998: 11–12). It is important to note here that the focus is not on the diagnosis of specific women. Rather, it is on discourses about women and madness and the relation to the social imaginary of drug users as the 'other'.

The signifier 'madness' is particularly problematic in relation to women in which typical characteristics of madness are those regarded to women. As Hockey (1993: 254) puts it, 'the apparently non-gendered profile of madness – passivity, emotionality, irrationality, dependency, lack of initiative, and need for support – is also a profile of a "normal" woman'. That is, women are socialised into these categories that are *per se* regarded as mental illness. Thus, accordingly, women who have a more independent or aggressive behaviour particularly concerning their social roles, risk psychiatric diagnosis, such as psychopathic or personality disordered. These aspects are central to the understanding of the imaginary of women who use drugs, in which addiction figures as incompatible with their social roles.

The signifier 'madness' operates on women in particular ways, in which 'natural madness' and 'vulnerability' of women was traditionally attributed to the female biology (Allen, 1986). Traditional 'medicine' portrayed women close to nature (including their reproductive functions) and sexuality (e.g. via menstruation), with the brain said to be driven by instincts (both sexual and maternal) (Rohden, 2003), contradiction, unpredictability, amorality and madness. This contrasts with men, in whom madness tends to be regarded as a consequence of deviance of social roles attributed to them (Engel, 1997). These ideas are reflected in women's traditional social roles related to the domestic sphere (children, marriage and motherhood), whereby discourses on the female physiology produce a scientific rationale that assigns them to nature and the domestic space, ensuring their inferiority in relation to men (Littlewood, 1994).

Emotionality and incapability to cope with social responsibilities are correspondingly addressed to women. This argument can be seen, for example, in the advertisements for tranquillisers where, as Littlewood (ibid.: 84) notes, women are portrayed as suffering from 'diffuse emotional symptoms' while men experience 'discrete episodes of anxiety'. These 'male' symptoms are related to specific circumstances of pressure at work or with a physical disease, contrary to women whose symptoms are related to 'nature'.

It is interesting to note that hysteria was considered a female feature, seen as a 'perverse femininity' (ibid.). Women's attributed 'mystery', has particular effects in this context, where the 'mysterious' woman seems to evoke both romantic and paranoid fantasies. This is seen, for example, in ideas of the nineteenth century in which aggression would come from seductive tactics (Haaken, 2002).

It is relevant to point out how this imaginary operates in drug discourses where women were said to be seducing men to use drugs (see Chapter 3). For example, considering the beauty product *Opium* by its name, these seductive tactics could be seen in the advertisement for *Opium* perfume (Yves Saint Laurent), in which the vamp (also an image accorded to drug users) woman appears to be seducing others to use opium. It is also interesting to note the contrast between the male and female portrayal of *Opium*, the pale white, vamp looking woman vs. the healthy, relaxed man.[1]

Furthermore, 'badness' or aggression is often seen as being inappropriate for women, incompatible qualities to what is expected from women, and in this sense, this imaginary of female fragility somehow implies the need for a protector. In the words of Haaken (ibid.: 8), 'femininity implied a fragile vulnerability that required a vigorously aggressive husband/protector'.

It is important to point out that, for specific social contexts and considering intersections between race and class, this image may not apply. For example, it might not extend to working class women or black women who are already marked as deviating from 'femininity'. Within the UK context, African Caribbean women have always had to be part of the labour market. In fact, Campbell (2000) emphasises the bias in women's research, in which white, middle class, and married women with children are portrayed as 'less at risk' or not visible in research.

In this sense, madness can function as a replacement for badness, whereas aggression for men is more socially acceptable than for women. This discursive construction produces specific effects, such as hasty diagnosis of mental illness for women who present aggressive behaviour. Indeed, women are more likely to be detained in psychiatric divisions than are men in the criminal system (Warner, 1996). Further, it has been highlighted that there is an increased number of women involved in drug trafficking (in high risk and low status roles, Harper *et al.*, 2002) and that imprisoned women are over stigmatized in a number of countries. Bush-Baskette (2004) points out the need for attention in the number and differences in incarceration of Black women (in the US).

Drug use by women is often regarded as a deviation of their social stereotypes, in which they are seen as unfeminine. This contrasts with men who are expected to be aggressive and self-indulgent (I further explore this in the section 'savage'). Characteristics such as:

> Educational maladjustment, disorderly behaviour, lack of emotional ties, illicit drug use and sexual activity outside marriage: all of these breach the expectation of conventional femininity, and in young women provide evidence that she is a psychopath. In a male, however, they may be acknowledged as socially deviant, but they are still consistent with the expectations of masculine normality, and are therefore treated as no more than ordinary delinquency.
>
> (Allen, 1987: 90 in Warner, 1996: 102)

Hence, drug addiction is seen as incompatible with expectations on women. In previous research (Mountian, 2004a), interviewees pointed out that women who are drug users are seen as suffering from psychological problems and as being sexually available. Women's sexuality was also seen as socially monitored, where women fear stigmatisation of sexual availability and/or madness (Mountian, 2007). Forth-Finegan (1991) also highlights some stereotypes around women alcoholics, which says that 'they are sicker and harder to treat than men' and points out sexist attitudes in all sections of the treatment.

Medical discourses on biological weakness of women are also important in discussions in this field. Although I do not deny functional biological differences between women and men, it is relevant to highlight how discourses on biological differences operate. Similarly, Campbell (2000) argues that 'biological vulnerability' to addiction, seen in terms of hormones and neurotransmitters, covers up gender bias and other social hierarchical divisions (such as race, ethnicity, sexuality and class). Moreover, Wright (2002) points out that, while there are biological differences between women's and men's bodies, such as distribution of fat tissue and hormonal changes, the impact of these biological factors is still under-researched.

Discourses on physiological effects of drugs on women, seen as poison or natural disaster, tend to naturalise gender differences. As seen in Chapter 3, by the end of the nineteenth century and beginning of the twentieth century, the idea that women were more prone to addiction than men had gained circulation. It is relevant to point out that this specific imaginary functions differently for different drugs, as is the case for psychiatric drugs, in which women are still more prescribed psychiatric drugs than men, while for other drugs, the recreational use 'does not fit into the stereotype of a "proper lady"' (Babcock, 1996: 2).

It is relevant to further analyse discourses on the physical and psychological weakness of women. Psychological weakness can be seen in terms of uncontrollability (of body and mind) and emotional responses. These discourses range from drug use to sexuality, and often appear intertwined. For example, in the following contemporary images of beauty advertisements, if we read these images from the perfume *Opium* (Yves Saint Laurent, in circulation from the 1980s onwards) as result of opium use, the contrast between these two sets of images seems suggestive.[2]

Contrasting these images, it seems that they operate according to the logic of biological and psychological weakness, so reproducing the idea of women as weaker, out of control (also sexually out of control), or sometimes unconscious after 'use', while men are posing for the picture in a calm, relaxed and controlled way. Furthermore, it is interesting to note the sexual connotation embedded in these images, although in both sets of images both women and men appear seductive, men seem to be in control, while women appear as being out of control (psychological weakness), somehow connected to sexual availability and vulnerability.

Dependency

During the 1920s, drugs were seen as jeopardising society, and young women were thought to be most at risk of forming drug habits. Fear of inter-marriage was at stake, by the seduction by men of colour facilitated by drug use (Kohn, 1992). This applied not only to discourses of abduction or forced prostitution, but to emancipated women as well (McDonald, 1994).

Reflecting on this xenophobic fear of seduction by men of colour, two aspects are emphasised: the symbolic position of women in relation to the nation's purity and morality (which I elaborate on in the following sub-section), and the social imaginary of sexual vulnerability and promiscuity 'triggered' by the use of drugs.

Discourses on drug use evoke ideas such as dependency (as opposed to self-control), moral weakness and immaturity, and the drug user is seen as 'infantile', dependent (as the classification of drug dependency itself), 'spontaneous' or not being able to postpone pleasure. These qualities are often seen as feminised, as Young (1971: 53) suggests: 'the undersocialised drug taker is seen in Freudian terms to have a weak superego, an inadequate ego – of a man – lack of proper masculine identification'. Juxtaposing these categories with gender, we can see that discourses on drug users are often those designated to women, that is, weak, immature, infantile, spontaneous, not able to postpone pleasure, irrational, emotional and dependent.

Thus, in explicitly gendering drug use, we can unravel discourses on the drug user (addict) as (1) that of the weak, of lacking in masculinity, characteristics often already conferred on women; and (2) on the paradoxical discourse of drug taking, in which drug use is regarded as a 'strong', 'macho' attitude. In this way, the focus on female drug users shows that these discourses operate ambiguously, that is, although dependency and weakness are often related to women (who are seen as more prone to addiction), women on drugs are regarded as *not feminine enough*, evoking deviant identifications of femininity such as the 'sick woman', the 'fallen woman', the 'bad woman' (Karsten, 1993). Furthermore, it is precisely these discourses that provide the scope for drug taking being seen as a challenge to social stereotypical roles, as further elaborated in this chapter.

Clearly, different drugs are associated with different images (e.g. tranquillisers, heroin) and relations to gender. For example, in the advertisement of cigarettes (in the US and Australia), '"mild" and "light" cigarettes are regarded as "feminine" as opposed to "strong" and "macho" cigarettes' (Jacobson, 1986).

In this sense, heroin use is predominantly regarded as part of male culture (Henderson, 1999), which is also related to the symbolism of needle usage. Indeed, Young (1994) points out that this is a male feature that appears to contrast with the 'soft' hippie world. It was noted by researchers that the practice of men injecting women prompts a discourse where addiction is seen as being less than if she was injecting herself (ibid.). Similarly, Wright (2002) points out that the stereotypical idea that women are initiated into drugs by their partners is challenged by women who have an active role in their initiation.

It is important to further conceptualise dependency in relation to gender. Dependency is typically regarded as an undesirable quality, not productive. This becomes particularly problematic when it is juxtaposed with gender, whereby women are socialised into dependency. As Ussher (1998: 151) highlights, 'in the traditional discursive construction of heterosexuality, "man" is positioned as powerful, and "woman" as passive and beholden to man'.

Indeed, Ettorre (1989: 103) reminds us of the origin of the word 'dependency', from the Latin *de pendere*, means to hang down from, 'defined as "a subordinate thing" as well as "addiction"'. In the analysis of 'dependency' and control, it is argued that the social expectation for women is to behave in the traditional way, that is, as dependent. However, Ettorre (ibid.: 105) suggests there is a logical incompatibility between 'the social expectation for women to be dependent and the need for all women to be "in control"'. In this way, at the same time that there is this imaginary of uncontrollability and emotional spontaneity of women, it is expected for women to be in control.

Nation

Focusing on the symbolic position of women in relation to nation, it is possible to point out that women are typically seen as the representative of the social order, the 'keepers' of society's morality, having the traditional social roles of mothers and carers. Yuval-Davis (1997: 2) argues that women 'reproduce nations, biologically, culturally and symbolically'. However, this is a paradoxical position in which, although women are essentially part of nation, they are not included in the political arena, since the private sphere is not considered politically relevant. McClintock (1995: 359) makes a similar point, stating that 'women are typically constructed as the symbolic bearers of nation, but are denied any direct relation to national agency'. So, at the same time that women are located outside the public realms and political decisions, they are the representatives of cultural moralities, they reproduce, maintain and symbolise the 'motherland'.

It is important to highlight here that the term 'nation' must be historically situated (in the same way as gender). As Yuval-Davis (1997: 4) asserts, 'nations are situated in specific historical moments and are constructed by shifting discourses promoted by different groupings competing for hegemony'. The signifier 'nation' operates in different ways according to specific social and political contexts. The word 'nation', coming from *natio*, to be born, is spoken as 'motherland' and 'fatherland' (McClintock, 1995). In this sense, 'family' is a crucial metaphor for nation:

> A curious paradox emerged. The family as a metaphor offered a single genesis narrative for national history while, at the same time, the family as an institution became void of history and excluded from national power. The family became, at once and at the same time, both the organising figure for national history and its antithesis.
>
> (ibid.: 357)

During the nineteenth century, family and nationalism were very much linked. The subordination of women to men was conceived of as natural, so hierarchies of nation were portrayed in familial terms warranting their 'natural' social position. Within this dynamic, McClintock (ibid.) analyses the discursive position of gender within nation, in which women are seen as backwards and conservative, while men are progressive and revolutionary:

> Women are represented as the atavistic and authentic body of national tradition (inert, backward-looking and natural), embodying nationalism's conservative principle of continuity. Men, by contrast, represent the progressive agent of national modernity (forward-thrusting, potent and historic), embodying nationalism's progressive, or revolutionary principle of discontinuity.
>
> (ibid.: 359)

It is interesting to note the temporal location of women in McClintock's account, in which women are seen as existing in an archaic time, as the colonised nations, contrasting with the modern white middle class men.

It is important to highlight the position of women as cultural reproducers of nation, especially for older women, in which the role of cultural reproducers is given to them and should dictate their appropriate behaviour, and this role of representation functions at both individual and collective levels (Yuval-Davis, 1997). This place of women as moral agents is also derived from that of the (feminised) body politics, the nation's mother and healthy children 'to ensure a strong imperial race' (McDonald, 1994: 22).

Within this symbolic position accorded to women in relation to nation, drug use configures a special threat to nation, family and women themselves, in the same way as homosexuality, prostitution and obscenity (Warner, 1996). Adding to this, within this space of moral symbolisation, in which women are expected to be in control, their space for indulgence is limited, subject to surveillance and control.

This symbolic position that women occupy and these particular discourses of women who use drugs, concerning madness and moral degradation, produce a particular highly feared and stigmatised arena. Here, we can see the production of an imaginary of women as both victims and/or a threat to society. This can be seen, for example, in discourses of keeping away from drugs (including alcohol) in the name of nation and in the name of family. Furthermore, it is important to point out discursive associations between using drugs and racial inter-marriage (e.g. with people of colour, the colonised), as threatening the nation (reflecting, among other issues, a biological understanding of nation).

Threat

Discourses on the drug user as a threat (as 'plague') portrays the user as criminal, evil and immoral. Focusing on women, some important gender differences emerge, particularly in relation to discourses on madness and sexuality, in which the 'savagery' of women is typically substituted by 'madness' and/or 'immorality' (connecting with sexual 'immorality'). Three aspects are highlighted here: first, the contrast of the image of men as violent, and women as sexually immoral and/or 'mad'; second, discourses on women's sexuality and the relation with control; and third, the debate over the (in)visibility of women's drug use in relation to their social roles.

Public woman vs. woman in public

Women's drug use somehow functions as a catalyst for fears and draws on a specific imaginary in relation to women's sexual desires. In this section, I analyse these stereotypical images: women in public (as prostitutes or lesbians) and in private (as mothers). Before embarking on this, it is important to note that I do not deny the existence of women (and men) sex workers who may use drugs, or that prostitution may also exist as a way to support one's habit (Karsten, 1993). However, the objective is to look at how these discourses inform mainstream images of women and drugs.

Traditionally, women's acceptable social roles were mainly related to reproduction and caring for the children, husband and family. Women were portrayed according to two opposite images, that is, the mother and the prostitute. 'The positive pole shows the woman on a pedestal, the woman as Madonna; the negative pole typifies the woman who has failed, the "fallen woman", the prostitute' (ibid.: 6). Prostitution was typically seen as abnormal, self-destructive and a threat to society.

Analysing these two images, the 'mother' and 'fallen woman', psychoanalysis brings some further insights. By being posited at the margin in discourse, the feminine represents what is symbolised or not, what can be controlled and what can be subverted. Moi (2010: 166), drawing on Kristeva, argues that, within Western culture, women came to represent the limit between man and chaos, being placed neither inside nor outside, not known or unknown, giving rise to the creation of two basic discursive formations: the dark and chaotic (Lilith or the whore of Babylon), or to be venerated as being pure and close to nature (Virgins and Mothers of God). In this sense, Frosh (1995: 295) points out, 'whichever tendency dominates, "woman" here is a product of imagination, literally the imaginary; a fantasy that holds masculinity in place'.

Aspects of the imaginary of women in relation to drug use circulate around particular repetitive feminine positions in discourse, and at the intersection of drug use and gender, images of the 'fallen woman' re-emerge. In Chapter 3, I discussed how, in the 1920s, ideas of prostitution operated in relation to drug use in the UK and US. During this period, important changes were occurring in society, including women's appearance in public without the company of men, and smoking in public. This could be regarded as a challenge to the public image of women, in which 'a "public woman" was a prostitute' (Kohn, 1992: 52). These ideas can still be seen in some contemporary discourses on women and drug use, particularly on women who are seen unaccompanied in some places at specific times of the day/night (e.g. streets, bars, etc.).

Discursive intersections between women and drugs are seen to highly operate around moral sexual realms, whereby deviance for women is frequently discursively connected to sexual deviance. A number of works have pointed out this particular social imaginary. For example, Padayachee (2002) comments on Johnson's (1965) research on doctors: 'it was revealed that doctors believed that alcoholic women had loose sexual morals, had more psycho-sexual conflicts and were more likely to get into social difficulties than men', and Finkelstein (1996: 33) highlights that women drug users and drinkers are often associated with 'rampant sexuality', as indicated by the use of terms such as 'tramp', 'lush' and 'whore'. In this sense, the image of female drug users is reiterated as a symptom of female deviance, that is, prostitutes or lesbians, expressed in ideas such as 'not behaving as girls' or 'not behaving as proper girls' (Campbell, 2000: 154).

This was also seen in previous research (Mountian, 2004a, 2007) where interviewees pointed out ideas such as 'women have to prostitute to use drugs', or 'when she is high she can sleep with anyone', 'sexually available', 'bitch', 'it's worse to see a woman on drugs than men'. Stealing was not mentioned as a possible act for women.

Within this context, deviance is typically seen as deviance from sexual roles. In this way, it is interesting to note the sexualised connotation in gender performances in relation to drugs. Jacobson (1981: 41) points this out in relation to cigarette smoking, whereby for boys cigarette smoking is also part of the image expected from them. 'It is an image that says: "I'm cool and daring; I've had sexual experience"', while this image does not extend to women, who are expected to be 'quiet, demure and cooperative' (ibid.: 41).

From previous research (Mountian, 2004a), similar images were emphasised and comparisons made with sexual activity. A woman who has different partners or uses drugs was said to be a 'bitch', contrary to men for whom it was seen as an expected activity. It also emphasised the importance for women to not use drugs, including cigarettes, to smell nice, be quiet and respect their husbands. Further, some male drug users expressed disgust at women who use drugs. These examples highlight a specific social imaginary of women, more precisely what is expected from women ('respect her husband', 'be quiet') and how these intersect with drug taking. That is, a 'proper woman' does not take drugs (recreationally).

The 'strangeness' of women taking drugs is also highlighted by O'Bryan's (1989) study of young people and drug use in inner north London. O'Bryan points out that the young male group interviewed regarded taking heroin as being 'hard' and 'able to take it', and they disapproved the use of heroin by girls. 'Any girls who had tried the drug were uniformly described as "slags", a term of sexual abuse groups of men often reserve for women whom they feel have broken the limits of "acceptable ladylike behaviour"' (ibid.: 66).

Further, it is relevant to note the discursive location of 'desire' for this social imaginary of the 'proper lady', where the term 'need' fits better. Littlewood (1994) highlights discursive binaries such as culture vs. nature, male vs. female, active vs. passive, and desire vs. need, among others. Within these divisions, 'need' was seen to be more suitable for women, since 'desire' presupposes a more active and aggressive role, also reminiscing the longstanding debate between need and free will in drug addiction.

The social expectation of 'behaving like a proper girl' is an important aspect for the imaginary of women and drugs, evoking the polarised images of 'public woman' and 'woman in public', or in some contexts, that of the lesbian.

Visibility

The dynamics of visibility and invisibility in relation to women's drug taking accord to the social imaginary of the woman drug user. This explicitly or implicitly circulates around sexual realms, in which the (culturally masculine) gaze in relation to women is (hetero) sexually oriented.

Foucault's (1991) analysis of mechanisms of power is relevant here: the traditional form of power (visibility) and the disciplinary power (invisibility) (see Chapter 5). Traditional power deployed by force was what was seen, shown and manifested. 'Those on whom it was exercised could remain in the shade' (ibid.: 187). While disciplinary power 'is exercised through its invisibility; at the same time it imposes on those whom it subjects a principle of compulsory visibility' (ibid.: 187). Under this disciplinary power, the subjects are those who are seen, and it is exactly through their visibility that power is exercised. 'The examination is the technique by which power, instead of emitting the signs of its potency, instead of imposing its mark on its subjects, holds them in a mechanism of objectification' (ibid.: 187).

Within this perspective, it is possible to point out how these two mechanisms (traditional and disciplinary) operate in relation to illegal drug use, and in the case of female drug users, how the process of objectification takes place. Hence, it is not surprising to find sexualised and gendered discursive dynamics in the social imaginary of women.

Within these mechanisms of power, the notion of the gaze, a surveillance that enables it to qualify, classify and punish, is crucial. In relation to the normative gaze over women, social boundaries for women are seen as clearer than for men, so transgression of these boundaries makes them more visible, bringing stigmatisation and ostracism. Paradoxically, the visibility of 'polluted women' can also represent a challenge to patriarchal society (being feared, she also has personal power). The visible junkie woman is seen as rejecting femininity, as a non-woman (prostitute, lesbian), while the invisible 'polluted' woman (e.g. on tranquillisers) is seen as dependent, as a passive victim (mothers, mothers-to-be) (Ettorre, 1989). This dynamic is particularly important to the field of women and drugs, since it produces specific practices, such as the solitary domestic use of drugs.

It is interesting to note how these stereotypical images of women and drugs are portrayed in films. For example, on the images of drugs and prostitution, in the movie *Traffic* (Steven Soderbergh, 2000), an upper class teenage girl becomes a kind of 'unconscious' prostitute for her drug use, which contrasts with her male friend who introduced her to drugs but manages to carry on with his studies and his life without big structural changes. Another stereotype (among many) in this movie is that the mother of the girl self-medicates.

The movie *Requiem for a Dream* (Darren Aronofsky, 2000) is also suggestive here, in which the men end up in prison, the woman becomes a prostitute to support her drug habit, and the mother enters a psychiatric hospital for her use of pills for slimming (amphetamines). Another aspect that appears in both movies is that both prostitution and drugs are managed by black men, reproducing social stereotypes around race. Within these examples, I emphasise the image of the young girl and illegal drug use connected with prostitution (public space), and the mother's consumption of legal drugs at home (domestic sphere).

These images also evoke the difference of drug taking according to age. In previous research (Mountian, 2004a), it was seen how the culture of drinking for women is changing. Where in the past it was not acceptable for women to drink and it was emphasised by the interviewees that women should drink little, usually accompanied and should get a less strong drink (sweet and colourful drinks are often regarded as drinks for women), she should in fact drink to make company for men, and should never get drunk in public because it is regarded as 'ugly', shocking and unfeminine. Indeed, as Ettorre (1989: 109) also notes, 'the pursuit of pleasure for women makes them feel selfish, unfeminine, not nice'.

Another crucial aspect regarding women drinking and past generations refers to the role of emotions such as shame and shyness derived from the transgressing character of pleasure for women. An older woman would prefer to drink (and use other drugs) at home, so she is not seen drinking in public. This brings another set of effects; she becomes invisible, isolates herself, and may only become visible when developing a drinking problem. Further, at times, the group can function to regulate drug use, and this invisibility of domestic use of drugs can be harder to reach for drug policies.

Ettorre (ibid.: 105) points out some images of 'polluted women' in private and public spheres. In private these women 'are seen as potentially "sexless", bad mothers, uncaring for their children or irresponsible wives, not considering the needs of their husbands'. In public, they are 'viewed as unforgivably out of control in their domestic and/or work situations, "evil sluts" or "loose women", who cannot be trusted and should be avoided' (ibid.: 105). This can also be seen in the stigmatisation and marginalisation of women, and particularly on pregnant women who use drugs (including cigarettes and alcohol).

The dynamics of visibility and invisibility also differs according to forms of drug taking and types of drugs, such as the use of tranquillisers or alcohol at home, in contrast to smoking, drinking or taking illegal drugs in public. The division between private and public spaces is key here.

Invisibility

Regarding the invisible 'polluted' woman, we should note the high rate of psychotropic drugs prescribed for women. Advertisements for minor tranquillisers and antidepressants (for psychotropic drugs) are more frequent for women, whereas for other medications there is a greater presence of men (Littlewood, 1994). Furthermore, in these advertisements in general, women appear as housewives or looking after the children. In the same vein, Herzberg (2009) highlights adverts of psychotropic drugs, particularly minor tranquillisers and antidepressants in the broad media, and it is still the case that these advertisements portray the familiar picture of the middle class white woman, the most prescribed group. Herzberg also highlights the second-wave feminist movement's position against the 'mother's little helper'. The discourse of motherhood (e.g. mothers or women as mothers-to-be) plays an important role for the imaginary of women and dynamics of drug use.

It is relevant to point out how discourses on controllability function according to the context and to the specific substances utilised, such as in the difference between legal and illegal drugs (Prozac, ecstasy). For example, tranquillisers for white women have been regarded as a way to keep them calm and caring for the family in circumscribed control. Within these discourses, motherhood is regarded as woman's destiny and, as such, there is a range of expected behaviours such as unconditional love, care, self-sacrifice, and no scope for ambivalent feelings (Lewis, 2002). It is also possible to reflect on how these drugs can be used for coping strategies, that is, to be in control.

A number of questions are at stake here: are women more prescribed antidepressants because the pressures are higher on them, functioning as a way of social control, or as a way of being in control? Further, how do discourses on women contribute do this over-prescription, particularly on the psychology of women, that is, as the 'enigmatic' character of women, which is frequently naturalised in the social functions of mothers and carers, and on discourses on their physiology (pre-menstrual tensions, hormone-craze, etc.)?

Within this interdiction of pleasure, it is also possible to see the use of drugs regarded as therapeutic aid or as coping strategies, in which pleasure plays a secondary role, drawing on the idea that 'need' is more suitable for women than pleasure. Previous research (Mountian, 2004a), discusses the use of drugs as a coping strategy, for example using alcohol as a way of dealing with personal relationships and domestic housework. In this way, Wright (2002) points out that the attribution of life problems can be a strategy to deflect censure. In the same vein, Blackburn and Graham (1992: 1) suggest that cigarette smoking is now usually associated with young, white, working class women, particularly those with children, where cigarettes appear as coping strategies for their social circumstances.

Girl power

Smoking illustrates well key discourses around drugs, and specifically around women and drugs. At one time, smoking was not allowed or expected from women in many Western countries. Only in the 1920s did women start smoking in public and, until recently, women smoking were seen in some ways as daring, modern, glamorous and challenging. This image might be changing now with the anti-tobacco campaigns, which portray women as bad mothers, hazards for children and bad role models (for children). Notwithstanding this, there is still a social imaginary of women and smoking drawing on a challenge or rejection of stereotypical images of women, as Jacobson (1981: 41) notes: 'they can be as rebellious, daring and anti-establishment as boys'. Indeed, this image was particularly explored by tobacco companies, whose advertisements drew on themes such as power, freedom and choice, which I examine next. The images utilised in this chapter are part of contemporary cigarette campaigns (1990s), and they were retrieved from www.tobaccofreekids.org/adgallery/ (2010). I also indicate in which country these advertisements appeared.

Power

Focusing on the image of daring and challenging social roles of women drug users, at times drawing on women's movements, here I highlight the notions of power and transgression. It is relevant to point out that power, rebellion and challenge also have a gender connotation, which play on stereotypical discourses that these are masculine traits. Figures 6.1 and 6.2 (p. 119) illustrate power in relation to smoking. In these specific images, this can be seen in the implicit idea of power gained by the entrance into the man's world.

The advertisement in Figure 6.1 shows the woman smoker entering a space that is typically reserved for men: 'snooker' (and smoking). Somehow, smoking allows her to have the necessary strength. Her leather trousers emphasise her sexuality, the male gaze subtly emphasises the image, and she is 'wearing the trousers'. In Figure 6.2 this entrance into the men's world is explicit.

In this advertisement, the woman is portrayed inside a space exclusively for men: the 'men's locker room'. By smoking, she gains entrance into the men's world, playing with the same rules. Moreover, it is interesting to note the utilisation of shyness, bringing the idea of defying the space reserved for women, as previously pointed out.

The advertisement in Figure 6.3 (p. 120), 'Share your happiness', shows a man entering the woman's world. It is interesting to note the specific world targeted in this advert: 'waxing', a painful technique utilised to enhance women's beauty. Further, considering the danger of feminised discourses, the dress code (swim suit) of the male, can be seen as safeguarding his masculinity, also supported by the flirtatious looks of women. Waxing in this image is stressed, not used for beauty purposes, but for a need (swimming). The male model is wearing swimming goggles and a swim suit in the hairdresser.

Choice and freedom

The idea of women's emancipation is stressed in Figures 6.4–6.8, which show images underlining choice and freedom. Two aspects are emphasised here: first, the idea of choice or free will to smoke, a notion that is usually the dispute in anti-tobacco campaigns that state that smokers are addicted, so not free. Second, when this is juxtaposed with gender, different connotations appear, in which smoking for women at times symbolises the possibility of choice and freedom in societal realms, as a mark of women's liberation.

In the Virginia Slims campaign (see Figure 6.4, p. 120), the slogan used is: 'I am able to decide on everything without saying a word. Virginia Slims: seek (find) your truth'. The power obtained by smoking is emphasised as a sort of liberation, in which she is able to decide on everything. However, there is a paradoxical message delivered by this advertisement, in which, on the one hand, she decides on everything and does not need to speak out, and, on the other hand, by not speaking out, she is kept in silence, reproducing the stereotypical social position of women. Further, it is possible to ask: why is there a need to stress 'I am able to decide'?

The cigarette campaigns shown in Figures 6.5 and 6.6 (p. 122) have the overt message 'I choose'. This underlines the idea of power in terms of the individual as the active agent. Power of choice is seen here in two aspects: choice of smoking cigarettes (opposing the concept of addiction) and the active role of choosing in other aspects of daily life, such as sexual partners. Hence, it is relevant to note how sexuality and gender are portrayed in these images.

Figure 6.1 Lucky Strike advert (woman playing snooker), United States.

Source: www.tobaccofreekids.org

Figure 6.2 Winston advert ('Do I look shy?'), South Africa.

Source: www.tobaccofreekids.org

Figure 6.3 L&M campaign ('Comparte tu Alegría), Spain.
Source: www.tobaccofreekids.org

Figure 6.4 Virginia Slims advert (publication Latina), United States.
Source: www.tobaccofreekids.org

In Figure 6.5 choice is related to power, with the woman appearing as sexually dominant. This is also supported by the sign 'women' behind (they are in a ladies toilet). In Figure 6.6 choice is related to the power of sexual choice.

In these Lucky Strike campaigns, freedom of choice is emphasised in relation to sexuality, in which sex is a place of power. Pleasure is regarded as transgressing for women, thus sex and drugs become highly stigmatised. As previously pointed out, the social imaginary of women and drugs operates on the idea of deviance in which discourses of prostitution, and at times of lesbianism, are evoked, as utilised in the image shown in Figure 6.6. Moreover, this particular image carries an ambiguous message, as it may also be appealing for a male audience.

In the campaigns illustrated in Figures 6.7 and 6.8 (p. 123), tattoos appear as a transgressing or rebelling mark. Here, choice is also related to having a tattoo, which is exposed in the man's back – a mark of lifestyle. It is interesting to note that tattoos also appear in some discourses as associated with drug use. Moreover, it is relevant to note how this contrasts with the following image, in which a sexual connotation is implied, making explicit gender relations.

In Figure 6.8, smoking is connected with the idea of rebelling, daring and challenging social stereotypes, which is also stressed by the fact that the woman has a tattoo. However, there is a particular gender position highlighted here in the sexual provocation of the sentence 'Yeah, I have a tattoo. And no, you can't see it', playing on an ambiguous position. At the same time that the woman is portrayed in this particular way, there is power in choosing not to show the tattoo.

The exotic

Race also plays an important role in the campaigns shown in Figures 6.9 and 6.10 (p. 124). Two aspects are highlighted: campaigns targeting specific cultural groups and the utilisation of discourses of race (and gender) as exotic.

Cigarette campaigns by Virginia Slims primarily target women. Virginia Slims is a thin cigarette with a white filter, that is, for women. In a similar way, representations are also found in cigarette campaigns portraying men, for example Marlboro, where the yellow filter and strong cigarettes are used to emphasise strength and masculine traits. In these particular advertisements from Virginia Slims, the idea of smoking is associated with women's liberation, where the motto is: 'find your voice'. Here, I emphasise the specifically racialised as well as gendered targets of these campaigns.

Figure 6.5 Lucky Strike campaign ('I choose', woman and man), Spain.

Source: www.tobaccofreekids.org

Figure 6.6 Lucky Strike campaign ('I choose', woman and woman), Spain.

Source: www.tobaccofreekids.org

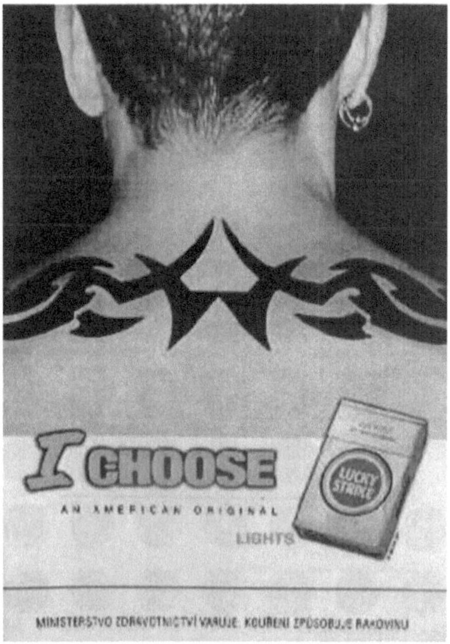

Figure 6.7 Lucky Strike campaign ('I choose', tattooed man), Czech Republic.

Source: www.tobaccofreekids.org

Figure 6.8 Winston advert ('Yeah, I have a tattoo. And no, you can't see it'), United States.

Source: www.tobaccofreekids.org

Figure 6.9 Virginia Slims advert ('Find your voice', black woman), United States.

Source: www.tobaccofreekids.org

Figure 6.10 Virginia Slims advert ('My voice reveals the hidden power within', Japanese woman), United States.

Source: www.tobaccofreekids.org

In Figures 6.9 and 6.10, it is possible clearly to see , on the one hand, the gendered target with the message 'Find your voice'. On the other hand, the racial element can be seen as playing in ambiguous ways, in which 'Find your voice' can also promote the idea that Western culture is liberated. 'My voice reveals the hidden power within' plays on stereotypical images of groups for the Japanese (Geisha) representation, while it is interesting to note the saying 'never let the goody two shoes get you down' in the advert portraying a black woman.

Pleasure

The images presented in this chapter as a whole draw on the idea of smoking as powerful and liberating. Pleasure for women is a transgressing category, and transgression, in this case, can be seen as a challenge to social stereotypes, related to freedom and rebellion. Nevertheless, it is important to emphasise that these images of women and men and drugs vary enormously according to the type of drug (i.e. prescribed, legal and illegal), quantity and frequency of consumption, and historical, social, political contexts, changing in relation to class, race, age and specific peer groups:

> Some drug-takers will of course have no special vocabulary at all (e.g., housewives who use barbiturates). This signifies that they are interpreting and structuring their experiences in terms of the wider culture to which they belong. Others, however, will evolve elaborated and sophisticated argots, which involve the genesis of alternative value systems and radical reinterpretations of 'reality' (e.g., hippies).
>
> (Young, 1971: 69)

Analysing the street language utilised for drugs, Young (1994: 65) notes that the street culture of addiction is highly grounded in masculine symbols:

> Evocative of a cold, technological style, which often reveals its own intimations of warfare and battle, and again places firmly in a culture of masculinity. The mechanistic 'fixing', jacking up with a set of works, getting a hit, blasting, making a score, crashing out or 'shooting a spoke' are all tinged with reflections of a male and sometimes sado-masochistic world. In such a cultural milieu, street-dealing in smack, crack, horse or 'snow' contains few of the allegedly feminine attributes of 'love, peace and communal caring'

which the symbolically feminine world of cannabis-use brought into the cultural world of the 'swinging 60s'.

In this sense, we can reflect on how the use of ecstasy in clubs from the 1990s seems to evoke rather different significations. Here, I focus on the club culture to elaborate on the image of the modern woman, the glamour involved in the club scene and the antagonistic discourses of women's emancipation. I begin by analysing images of advertisement for beauty products *Addict* (Dior) and *Crave* (Calvin Kein).[3]

In 2002, Dior launched a collection of beauty products for women called *Addict* and with the motto 'admit it'. After public reaction, Dior withdrew the motto 'admit it', but kept the label. This campaign from Dior provoked reactions, particularly from families of drug users. This kind of reaction also appeared in other beauty campaigns, such as *Opium* from Yves Saint Laurent, *Poison* from Dior, *Mania* from Giorgio Armani (trivialising depression) and *Obsession* from Calvin Klein.

Analysing these images of the beauty campaigns *Addict* (Dior) and *Crave* (Calvin Klein) two aspects are highlighted, particularly when contrasting these two images: sexual appeal and the idea of uncontrollability of women and drugs. *The Christian Science Monitor* (2002) writes: 'it pictured a slender model clothed mostly in beaded sweat with an anxious expression on her face, as if she needed a fix' (Faces and Voices of Recovery, 2003, www.facesandavoicesof recoverry.org/dior_news.htm), although the representation of 'needing of a fix' is overwhelmed by the specifically sexual characteristics of this image. Moreover, within the juxtaposition between the images of the *addict* woman and the *craving* man, the *addict* woman looks more craving, and sexually out of control than the *craving* man.

Hence, it is relevant to note how the image of emancipated women (who take drugs) plays dubiously in relation to sexuality, as also seen in previous research (Mountian, 2004a), where social stereotypes fall in terms of bitch, modern and irresponsible. Here, the quality of being modern is juxtaposed with the 'bitch' and 'irresponsible', ideas at times, associated in discourse.

The ambiguity of this social imaginary of women in the club scene is illustrated by this debate, while, on the one hand, the over-sexualised visibility of women and the reproduction of stereotypical social positions of women are seen in discourse; on the other hand, this provides a space for the discursive possibility of power and liberation of women as portrayed in these images, by defying pre-established rules. '*Addict* was created in homage to her liberation, to her open-mindedness and independence' (*Jerusalem Post,* 2002 in Faces and Voices of Recovery, 2003). 'She depends on nothing and on no one but herself. She opens her eyes, she focuses her mind and she lifts herself up. She comes, she goes and nothing will stop her.' The Dior website (dior-addict.com) describes it as follows: 'for strong, liberated women who like to be daring and disturbing'.

This *Addict* campaign from Dior alludes to the club scene, showing a woman dancing as if in the nightclub, with music and lights. In the club scene, these are important elements, where the glamorisation of drug use, dance, relaxation and fashion are highlighted. Henderson (1999) points out some gender relations in E-culture, where women are the insiders – 'the modern girl culture', and men produce rave music at home; although, it is still the case that most women participate as consumers, while men are the producers (participating as producers, DJs and promoters) (ibid.). However, the presence of women DJs and producers is increasing in the contemporary club scene. Interviews from previous research (Mountian, 2004a) pointed out that, in the space of nightclubs, there is a feeling of egalitarian communion, 'everybody is the same' (erasing differences based on class, gender, race and sexuality). Here, they argue, the goal is pleasure and fun.

Pleasure plays an important role in discourses of drug taking, however pleasure might take different forms in relation to gender. For example, for women it can be regarded as 'a subverted or hidden reality' (Henderson, 1999: 42), or as transgression to the moral symbolic function of women. Feminist research points out that 'given both the social and individual constraints placed upon women, our sexuality, and our bodies within a patriarchal society, real pleasure *for women* is impossible to attain' (Ettorre, 1989: 109).

When pleasure is connected with transgression, it can paradoxically be regarded as empowering and as a challenge to social roles, as seen in the analysis of cigarette adverts, in which smoking (pleasure) appears as transgressing social stereotypes in relation to gender. Within this limited space for indulgence addressed to women, discourses on 'need' may be more suitable than 'desire' for women, as previously pointed out. Two key aspects are worthy of emphasis: (1) pleasure as transgressive for women, and how emotions of shame and shyness play within this dynamic, and the effects of this sort of regulation, as the isolated domestic drug taking (drinking); and (2) pleasure functioning as a challenge to social stereotypes.

In this chapter, I have focused on aspects of the social imaginary of women and how this operates in relation to drug discourses. Key themes elaborated here were the imaginary of drug users in terms of notions of dependency, weakness, madness and (un)controllability, and how these function in relation to gender, considering the symbolic position of women in relation to nation.

Social stereotypical roles of women were highlighted as structuring specific imaginary formations, emphasising power in terms of visibility, invisibility and pleasure. Drawing on highly sexualised imaginary of women, two poles were identified: mothers or mothers-to-be, and prostites and lesbians. In this way, the social imaginary of women drug users appeared somehow as pre-empted, oscillating only between these poles. The masculine trait of taking drugs was also emphasised, and this was referenced in terms of representations of lesbians, which is again a sexualised designation, as the mother (who is typically seen as asexual) and the 'fallen' woman (hypersexual). Moreover, from this position of women in discourse, in which space for indulgence is more limited, the use of drugs could paradoxically be seen as a challenge to social positions.

7 Drug policies

While this book does not specifically aim to analyse in detail prevalent drug policies, some aspects of drug policies are important to highlight. In general, mainstream drug policies overlook specificities of drug use and do not take gender into account, as well as other social structural differences (class, race, age, disability, sexuality) and particular social contexts. Drug policies and health policies will be decided according to current understandings of drugs, and as such these will tend to oscillate between punishment and treatment. Not taking into account power structures and social contexts, there is a risk of punishing specific groups, and/or individualising and pathologising subjects.

The focus on key historical aspects of discourses of drugs allowed us to grasp changes of meanings and significations of drugs and addiction. The passage from the nineteenth to the twentieth century was of major importance for the understanding of contemporary approaches to drug addiction, in which religious, medical and legal discourses were identified as key discursive approaches to drugs. The creation of addiction as a disease was seen to have its basis there. These discursive structures (medical, religious and legal) are not value-free, but rather they produce and reproduce moral standpoints, as played out within the understandings of the notions of free will and control.

Indeed, discourses of drugs are deeply embedded in a moralistic frame, frequently producing 'moral panics' (Ben-Yehuda, 1994), which reduces possibilities of analysis. In fact, in the case of drug policies, critical accounts are often read as being 'pro-drugs'. This moralistic standpoint evokes longstanding discourse binaries such as good and bad, natural and artificial, and pure and impure, which, as I have shown, also intersect with notions of class, race, gender and nation.

Drawing on Foucault's (1991) mechanisms of power (the plague and the panopticon), the position of drugs and drug users as the 'other' was reiterated, oscillating between plague (menace) and victim, in which drug policies function accordingly. So, when drugs are seen as related to cure, they are invested in and encouraged (evoking the notion of remedy, Derrida, 1997). When drugs are related to pharmacological pleasures, social intervention is required.

The analysis of drug policies such as 'just say no', 'no to drugs, yes to life' and 'war on drugs' came to appear as largely based on this social imaginary of drugs. These drug policies are assumed to reflect a universal consensus of what is good, not taking into account the specifics of the situations. In so doing, they miss out important aspects for health issues, such as providing information about drugs. This fits with the contemporary notion of ethics of human rights, as pointed out by Badiou (2001), in which human rights are based on a specific ethics that understands good and 'evil' as universal consensus, not accounting for specific social contexts.

Hence, in this book I have emphasised the importance of taking the social contexts and meanings of drug use into account. This could be seen in relation to the manipulability of the substances themselves in religious and medical use of drugs, and how drugs operate in specific social and political contexts.

Drug policy and gender

In terms of gender, lack of research that attends to gender has been emphasised (Ettorre, 1992; Karsten, 1993; McDonald, 1994; Babcock, 1996; Drabble, 1996; Campbell, 2000; Raine, 2001; Klee *et al.*, 2002; Padayachee, 2002; Wright, 2002), as well as specialised treatment centres for women, and sexual diversity for lesbians, gays, bisexuals, transvestites and transsexuals, who are many times stigmatised and discriminated (Ettorre, 2005). In terms of sexuality, research points out the need to understand LGBT people's use of illegal drugs, and the need to consider differences of use by lesbian women, gay men and transsexual people (Hoare and Moon, 2010). Services are often developed taking the male experience as normative (Forth-Finegan, 1991; Babcock, 1996; Raine, 2001; Wright, 2002).

As seen in this book, this is a relevant claim, since these groups have differences in relation to their drug use and different forms of using – therapeutic use, fitness (Jacobson, 1981), different physical effects (e.g. the dangers of use of contraceptive pills and cigarettes, in which women smokers are more likely to have a heart attack or a stroke than a non-smoker, Jacobson, 1986), different meanings of using drugs such as coping strategies (Blackburn and Graham, 1992) (this does not apply only to women), and the effects of specific social imaginaries in relation to gender.

> Medical and psychological literature presented a picture of drug use in which drug users just happened to be male and women hardly figured. When they did, they appeared as sicker, more deviant, more psychologically disturbed than their male peers: as weak and pathetic creatures. Women's drug use figured as a "deviation" from "normal" femininity due to mental or physical deficiencies, or disease.
>
> (Henderson, 1999: 37)

However, attention turns to gender in drug treatment when it is directly related to its effects on others, such as childbirth and child rearing. In this sense, Campbell (2000: 25) argues that drug use is constructed as a 'form of violence that women commit against themselves and those closest to them'. Indeed, women's health or illness is very much connected to the idea of harming others, in which prostitution, pregnancy and child care are crucial aspects. In fact, HIV transmission impacted in services for women drug users, where there was a growth of policy and research (Henderson, 1999).

Further, research highlights that women with HIV are often more stigmatised than men, and if they are drug users, stigmatisation increases, in which they are seen as promiscuous and deviant. Klee (2002: 4) elucidates this:

> Reactions to women using drugs are generally negative in all nations but risks of drug-induced damage to the child, combined with transmission to them of HIV, resulted in public actions in the US that resembled mediaeval witch hunts in Europe . . . Crack mothers were demonised; it was widely reported that they were indifferent to their children or directly abusive.

Hence, stereotypical images of female drug users were revitalised in media, and punitive actions were taken (e.g. crack mothers). Again, as argued throughout this book, it is a claim that each case should be seen in detail, in its specificity, as of course many women who use drugs do take care of their children, as well as fathers. However, because of this general stigmatising view around women, policies are often too prompt to punish female drug users. These discourses have material effects and support actions such as the sterilisation of women (and men) drug users in the US and the UK (Project Prevention.org, 2010). As also highlighted by Campbell (2000: 139):

> While in the past women addicts who were pregnant or mothering were constructed as poor mothers who violated feminine norms by dominating their households, in the latter decades of the century women who biologically 'reproduced' addiction played stunningly demonised roles.

These discourses are also imbued in the idea that women drug users cannot control themselves; therefore, they cannot educate their children, and so – given women's roles in relation to nation – contribute to producing an unruly society.

Campbell (ibid.) analyses discourses of drug policies regarding women, in which childcare plays a central role. During the 1980s and 1990s, policy makers drew on the idea of the 'vulnerable child' or the 'foetus', positioning women either as victims or as 'victimisers', and deciding therefore on punitive or treatment drug policies. In this way, two perspectives in drug policy were arrived at: either the expansion of health and social apparatus or the punitive approach. 'Proponents of foetal rights use drug policy as a means to an end, a way to justify limiting women's rights while expanding a culturally conservative agenda' (ibid.: 139). Hence, a woman's responsibility for her foetus is at stake here: it is she who damages it by taking drugs (illegal drugs, cigarettes and alcohol). This model draws on an individualistic approach, in which society, including the father, does not share child-rearing responsibilities, as if the woman is raising her child in a social vacuum.

A key discourse identified was the 'decline of maternal instinct' as the source of policy problem. This called for a public surveillance, in which each citizen has the moral obligation of preventing mothers or future mothers from taking drugs (this is a common attitude, for example, in cigarette smoking and drinking, where passers by feel the moral space to intervene and ask the woman, and particularly pregnant women, to quit smoking or drinking). One of the effects of this call is that this can be used to deny women's autonomy over their bodies and lives.

Further, it is relevant to understand mainstream discourses on 'maternal instinct' and the discursive effects these reproduce. Maternal instinct here refers to a specific social position of women, in which they are mothers, or mothers-to-be, and they should be 'naturally' protective, emotional and look after children, husband, elderly people in the family, and the sick. When reproduction and domestic labour (Benhabib and Cornell, 1987) are the *only* possibilities for women, other positions in discourse are not allowed, denying women's body autonomy, and finally their choices.

Moreover, it is crucial to take into account the different social imaginaries of the female drug user, whereby still, in many Western countries, women who use drugs are typically seen as psychologically inadequate, passive, isolated, and not capable of coping with responsibilities (Henderson, 1999). These images are connected with the social stereotypical role of women at home: housework, child care and emotional support. Thus, the female illegal drug user is seen as rejecting this role and not capable of performing it.

These discourses contribute to the extra stigmatisation of women (Drabble, 2001; Klee, 2002), and this can produce different forms of drug taking, such as isolated domestic use of drugs (e.g. medical drugs, alcohol, illegal drugs). Klee (2002) points out that the social isolation of women drug users increases during pregnancy, bringing different sets of problems. This social stigma can operate as social sanction, preventing women (and men) from seeking out help (Weisner and Scmidt, 1992 in Babcock, 1996; Murphy and Rosenbaum, 1999; Klee, 2002; Wright, 2002), bringing the dynamics of (in)visibility, such as of 'alcoholics invisible' (Padayachee, 2002). This is key for social policies, as women may not feel safe to look for help because of further consequences (such as losing their children, stigmatisation, ostracism). Hence, Young (1994: 72) identifies the invisibility of women from the police perspective. For example, overdose is commonly regarded as an

> aberrant female activity, linked to ideas and symbolism rooted in the realms of 'domestic/personal failure' or feminine ineptitude. However, when the statistical record of those taking overdoses, for example, is assessed for criminality – officially and historically, a street-visible public event – the female once again vanishes from the scene.

Another key aspect structuring the realms of gender and drugs is the relation between domestic violence and drug use (e.g. alcohol), in which women are a common target (Velleman *et al.*, 1998). It is important to consider, as McDonald (1994) also notes, that behaviour is learnt, and as such, drunken behaviour is learnt as well. Therefore, it is fundamental to research and conceptualise aggressive male behaviour towards women (and contextualise it in relation to patriarchal societies) and its relationships with drug use.

The intersection of gender and drugs actually carries a political standpoint that calls for social structural changes. It is important to note that drugs policy is driven by a 'law and order' agenda, and this also appears to have a public/private split, in that drug policies are chiefly concerned with criminality and violence on the streets rather than in the domestic sphere. So, violence against women in the home, which may be linked to substance misuse, is frequently overlooked. Drug policies and provision need to be able to connect better with issues of domestic violence and women drug use.

Indeed, it is fundamental to drug policies that they become women-oriented (Ettorre, 1989; Bepko, 1991; Drabble, 1996; Raine, 2001) and draw on a perspective that includes women as '"social actors" rather than passive subject of power' (Henderson, 1999: 42). These aspects related to women should also be further expanded to attend to the intersectional character of women's positions, thus also encompassing current gaps in policy and provision around race (Littlewood and Lipsedge, 1989; Aitken, 1996; Drabble, 1996; Mountian, 2005b; Beddoes *et al.*, 2010a), age (Raine, 2001), sexuality/LGBT/homosexuality/transexuality (Ettorre, 2005; Beddoes *et al.*, 2010b), class (Blackburn and Graham, 1992), and disability (Beddoes *et al.*, 2010c).

Concluding comments

From the ethical perspective adopted in this book, it is clear that it does not provide a prescriptive conclusion, as it is a claim that the policies should be developed accounting for the specifics of the situations. Rather, this work points to the importance of taking into account – in the sense of challenging – the specific social imaginary produced (and reproduced) for planning and delivery of drug policies. Moreover, in relation to the question of how particular contexts inform specific forms of intoxication, although I do not exhaust this question, I indicate how the social context seems to inform, at least partially, specific forms of intoxication.

The effects of prohibition and drug use have to be considered and further researched in relation to health issues and public policies: intoxication because of mixture, not control over the quality of the substance, ways of taking drugs, crime-related, war. The importance of providing information about drugs and also about overdose prevention (harm reduction initiatives) is also argued.

Thus drugs, gender and social imaginary have a long and intertwined history and geographical extension. I have attempted to draw attention to the separated as well as connected aspects, including some counter-examples to the norm, hegemonic and dominant drug discourses. I intend for this analysis to contribute further to the existing conceptual approaches that underline the ways drug policies perform a specific role within drugs, gender and drug use.

Notes

3 Historical discourses of drugs

1 *Reefer Madness* (1938) is known as the most famous of exploitation films. www.imagesjournal.com/issue08/features/exploitation/

6 Gender in the social imaginary of drugs

1 It is also interesting to note the contrast between the male and female portrayal of *Opium*, the pale white, vamp looking woman vs. the healthy, relaxed man.
http://tinyurl.com/74jv8wt
http://tinyurl.com/7c4o99y

2 If we read these images from the perfume *Opium* (Yves Saint Laurent, in circulation from the 1980s onwards) as a result of opium use, the contrast between these two sets of images seems suggestive.
http://tinyurl.com/7fwdyq4
http://tinyurl.com/7a52h63
http://tinyurl.com/7ms8wna
http://tinyurl.com/7jsxof5

3 I begin by analysing images of advertisement for beauty products *Addict* (Dior) and *Crave* (Calvin Klein).
www.imagesdeparfums.fr/Klein_Calvin/Crave.php
www.imagesdeparfums.fr/Dior/Dior_Addict.php

References

Acker, Caroline Jean (1996). 'From all-purpose anodyne to marker of deviance: physicians' attitudes towards opiates in the US from 1890 to 1940', pp. 114–132. In Potter, Roy and Teich, Mikulas (eds). Drugs *and Narcotics in History*. Cambridge: Cambridge University Press.

Ahmed, Sara (2003). *Affective Economies. Social Text* 79, vol. 22, no. 2, pp. 117–140. Durham, NC: Duke University Press.

Ahmed, Sara (2000). *Strange Encounters: Embodied Others in Post-Coloniality*. London: Routledge.

Aitken, Gill (1996). 'The present absence/pathologised presence of black women in mental health services', pp. 75–95. In Burman, Erica, Aitken, Gill, Alldred, Pam, Allwood, Robin, Billington, Tom, Goldberg, Brenda, Gardo-López, Angel (eds). *Psychology Discourse Practice: From Regulation to Resistance*. London: Taylor & Francis.

Allen, Hillary (1987). *Justice Unbalanced: Gender, Psychiatry and Judicial Decisions*. Milton Keynes: Open University Press.

Allen, Hilary (1986). 'Psychiatry and the construction of the feminine', pp. 85–111. In Miller, Peter and Rose, Nikolas (eds). *The Power of Psychiatry*. Cambridge: Polity Press.

Alvesson, Mats and Skoldberg, Kaj (2000). *Reflexive Methodology: New Vistas for Qualitative Research*. London: Sage.

Althusser, Louis (1985). *Freud e Lacan, Marx e Freud*. Rio de Janeiro: Graal.

André, Serge (1991). *O Que Quer Uma Mulher*, Zahar, Jorge (ed.). Rio de Janeiro: Jorge Zahar.

Anthias, Floya and Yuval-Davis, Nira (1996). *Racialized Boundaries: Race, Nation, Gender, Colour and Class and the Anti-Racist Struggle*. London: Routledge.

Arnao, Giancarlo (2002). *The Semantics of Prohibition*. Retrieved from *Drug Text* in 2002, available at www.drugtext.org/.

Babcock, Marguerite (1996). 'Does feminism drive women to drink? Conflicting themes'. *The International Journal of Drug Policy*, vol. 7, no. 3. Retrieved from *Drug Text* in 2002, available at www.drugtext.org/articles/96734.htm.

Badiou, Alain (2001). *Ethics: An Essay on the Understanding of Evil*. London: Verso.

Balibar, E. and Wallerstein, I. (eds) (2002). *Race, Nation, Class. Ambiguous Identities*. Verso: London.

Balibar, E. (1991). 'Is there a "neo-racism"?', pp. 17–28. In Balibar, E. and Wallerstein, I. (eds). *Race, Nation, Class. Ambiguous Identities*. Verso: London.

Barthes, Roland (1973). *Mythologies*. London: Paladin.

Batsleer, Janet and Humphries, Beth (eds) (2000). *Welfare, Exclusion and Political Agency*. London: Routledge.

Becker, Howard Saul (1963). *Outsiders: Studies in the Sociology of Deviance*. New York: The Free Press.

Beddoes, Diane, Sheikh, Sanah, Khanna, Mohini and Pralat, Robert (2010a). *The Impact Of Drugs on Different Minority Groups: A Review of the UK Literature Part 1: Ethnic Groups*. Office for Public Management. London: UK Drug Policy Commission.

Beddoes, Diane, Sheikh, Sanah, Pralat, Robert and Sloman, Jo (2010b). *The Impact Of Drugs on Different Minority Groups: A Review of the UK Literature Part 2: Lesbian, Gay, Bisexual and Transgender (LGBT) Groups*. Office for Public Management. London: UK Drug Policy Commission.

Beddoes, Diane, Sheikh, Sanah, Khanna, Mohini and Francis, Rob (2010c). *The Impact Of Drugs on Different Minority Groups: A Review of the UK Literature Part 3: Disabled People*. Office for Public Management. London: UK Drug Policy Commission.

Ben-Yehuda, Nachman (1994). 'The sociology of moral panics toward a new synthesis', pp. 201–220. In Comber, Ross (ed.). *Drugs and Drug Use in Society: A Critical Reader*. Kent: Greenwich Press.

Benhabib, Seyla and Cornell, Drucilla (eds) (1987). *Feminismo Como Crítica da Modernidade*. Rio de Janeiro: Editora Rosa dos Ventos.

Benitez, Fernando (2000). *Los Hongos Alucinantes*. Mexico: Ediciones Era.

Bepko, Claudia (1991). *Feminism and Addiction*. London: Howarth.

Berridge, Virginia (1989). 'Historical issues', pp. 20–36. In MacGregor, Susanne (ed.). *Drugs and British Society: Response to a Social Problem in the 1980s*. London: Routledge.

Berridge, Virginia and Edwards, Griffith (1987). *Opium and the People: Opiate Use in Nineteenth Century England*. London: Yale University Press and New Haven.

Bhabha, Homi K. (2010). *The Location of Culture*. London: Routledge.

Birdwell, Jonathan, Chapman, Jake and Singleton, Nicola (2011). *Taking Drugs Seriously: A Demos and UK Drug Commission Report on Legal Highs*. London: Demos.

Blackburn, Clare and Graham, Hilary (1992). *Smoking Among Working Class Mothers*. Final Report. Department of Applied Social Studies. Coventry: University of Warwick.

Bourdieu, Pierre (1977). *Outline of a Theory of Practice*. Cambridge: Cambridge University Press.

Browne, Kath and Nash, Catherine J. (eds) (2010). *Queer Methods and Methodologies: Intersecting Queer Theories and Social Science Research*. Surrey: Ashgate.

Bucher, Richard (1992). *Drogas e Drogadição no Brasil*. Porto Alegre: Artes Medicas.

Burman, Erica (2008). *Developments: Child, Image, Nation*. London: Routledge.

Burman, Erica (2003). *Discourse Analysis Means Analysing Discourse: Some Comments on Antaki, Billing, Edwards and Potter. 'Discourse Analysis Means doing Analysis: A Critique of Six Analytic Shortcomings'*. Retrieved from Discourse Analyses Online www.shu.ac.uk/daol/.

Burman, Erica (2000). 'Method, measurement and madness', pp. 49–79. In Holzman, Lois and Morss, John (eds). *Postmodern Psychologies, Societal Practice and Political Life*. London: Routledge.

Burman, Erica (1998). 'Deconstructing feminist psychology', pp. 1–29. In Burman, Erica (ed.). *Deconstructing Feminist Psychology*. London: Sage.

Bush-Baskette, Stephanie R. (2004). 'The war on drugs as a war against black women', pp. 185–194. In Chesney-Lind, Meda and Pasko, Lisa (eds). *Girls, Women and Crime: Selected Readings*. London: Sage.

Butler, Judith (1999). *Gender Trouble: Feminism and the Subversion of Identity*. London: Routledge.

Butler, Judith (1997). *Excitable Speech: A Politics of the Performative*. London: Routledge.

Butler, Judith (1993). *Bodies that Matter: on the Discursive Limits of Sex*. London: Routledge.

Campbell, Nancy (2000). *Using Women: Gender, Drug Policy and Social Justice*. London: Routledge.

Castoriadis, Cornelius (1997). *World in Fragments: Writings on Politics, Society, Psychoanalysis and the Imagination*. Stanford, CA: Stanford University Press.

Castoriadis, Cornelius (1991). *Philosophy, Politics, Autonomy: Essays in Political Philosophy*. Oxford: Odeon, Oxford University Press.

Castoriadis, Cornelius (1986). *Instituição Imaginária da Sociedade*. Rio de Janeiro: Paz e Terra.

Chantler, K. (2007). 'Border crossings: nationhood, gender, culture and violence'. *International Journal of Critical Psychology*, vol. 20, pp. 138–166.

Chomsky, Noam (1991). *Deterring Democracy*. London: Verso.

Christie, Nils (1986). 'Suitable enemy', pp. 42–54. In Bianchi, Herman and von Swaaningen, Rene (eds) *Abolitionism: Toward a Non-Repressive Approach to Crime*. Amsterdam: Free University Press.

Cixous, Helen (1976). 'The laugh of the Medusa'. *Signs*, vol. 1, no. 4, pp. 875–893.

Coomber, Ross (1998). *The Control of Drugs and Drug Users: Reason or Reaction?* Amsterdam: Harwood.

Coomber, Ross (1994). *Drugs and Drug use in Society: A Critical Reader*. Kent: Greenwich Press.

Cooperstock, Ruth and Parnell, Penny (2002). 'Research on psychotropic drug use: a review of findings and methods'. *Social Science and Medicine*, vol. 16, no. 12, pp. 1179–1196.

Courtwright, David T. (2001). *Forces of Habit: Drugs and the Making of the Modern World*. Cambridge, MA: Harvard University Press.

Courtwright, David T. (1995). 'The rise and fall and rise of cocaine in the United States', pp. 206–229. In Goodman, Jordan, Lovejoy, Paul and Sherratt, Andrew (eds). *Consuming Habits: Drugs in History and Anthropology*. London: Routledge.

Dally, Ann (1996). 'Anomalies and mysteries in the 'war on drugs', pp. 199–215. In Potter, Roy and Teich, Mikulas (eds). *Drugs and Narcotics in History*. Cambridge: Cambridge University Press.

Davies, John B. (1997). *The Myth of Addiction*. Amsterdam: Harwood Academic Publishers.

Dawson, C.R. (2003). *Drug Scoping Study: Asylum Seekers and Refugee Communities*. London: Home Office.

Dean, Hartley and Taylor-Gooby, Peter (1992). *Dependency Culture: The Explosion of a Myth*. London: Haverster Wheatsheaf.

Deleuze, Gilles e Guattari, Felix (1997). *Mil Platôs: Capitalismo e Esquizofrênia*. Rio de Janeiro: Editora 34.

Derrida, Jacques (2000 [1972]). *Disseminations*. London: Continuum Books.

Derrida, Jacques (1997). *A Farmácia de Platão*. São Paulo: Iluminuras.

Des Jarlais, Don (1995). 'Harm reduction: a framework for incorporating science into drug policy'. *American Journal of Public Health*, vol. 85, no. 1, pp. 10–11.

Dorn, Nicholas and Lee, Maggy (1999). 'Drugs and policing in Europe: from low streets to high places', pp. 86–102. In South, Nigel (ed.). *Drugs: Cultures, Controls and Everyday Life*. London: Sage.

Douglas, Mary (ed.) (1987). *Constructive Drinking: Perspectives on Drink from Anthropology*. Cambridge: Cambridge University Press.

Drabble, Laurie (1996). 'Elements of effective services for women in recovery: implications for clinicians and program supervisors', pp. 1–22. In Underhill, Brenda and Finnegan, Dana (eds). *Chemical Dependency: Women at Risk*. London: Harrington Press.

Drugscope (2011). Retrieved in 2011 from www.drugscope.org.uk.

Dunker, Christian (2011). *The Constitution of the Psychoanalytic Clinic*. London: Karnak.

Dunker, Christian (1996). *Lacan e a Clínica da Interpretação*. São Paulo: Hacker Editores and CESPuc and Fapesp.

Engel, Magali (1997). 'Psiquiatria e feminilidade', pp. 322–361. In Del Priore, Mary (ed.). *História das Mulheres no Brasil*. São Paulo: Editora Contexto.

Escohotado, Antonio (1998). *Historia de las Drogas*, vols. 1, 2 and 3. Madrid: Allianza Editorial.

Ettorre, Betsy (1989). 'Women, Substance Abuse and Self-Help', pp. 101–115. In MacGregor, Susanne (ed.). *Drugs and British Society: Responses to a Social Problem in the Eighties*. London: Routledge.

Ettorre, Elizabeth (ed.) (2005). *Making Lesbians Visible in the Substance Use Field*. Binghamton: Harrington Park Press.

Ettorre, Elizabeth (1992). *Women and Substance Use*. London: Macmillan.

Ettorre, Elizabeth and Riska, Elianne (1995). *Gendered Moods: Psychotropics and Society*. London: Routledge.

Evans, Dylan (1996). *An Introductory Dictionary of Lacanian Psychoanalysis*. London: Routledge.

Faces and Voices of Recovery (2003). www.facesandavoicesofrecoverry.org/dior_news.htm.

Fairclough, Norman (1995). *Critical Discourse Analysis: The Critical Study of Language*. London: Longman.

Fairclough, Norman (1992). *Discourse and Social Change*. Cambridge: Polity Press.

Fanon, Frantz (1986). *Black Skin, White Masks*. London: Pluto Press.

Feaster, Felicia and Wood, Bret (2002). 'The golden age of exploitation. An interview'. Retrieved from www.imagesjournal.com/issue08/features/exploitation/.

Finkelstein, Norma (1996). 'Using the relational model as a context for treating pregnant and parenting chemically dependent women', pp. 23–44. In Underhill, Brenda and Finnegan, Dana (eds). *Chemical Dependency: Women at Risk*. London: Harrington Press.

Forth-Finegan, Jahn L. (1991). 'Sugar and spice and everything nice: gender socialisation and women's addiction – a literature review', pp. 19–36. In Bepko, Claudia (ed.). *Feminism and Addiction*. London: Howarth.

Foucault, Michel (2002/1969). *The Archaeology of Knowledge*. London: Routledge.

Foucault, Michel (1998). *The Will to Knowledge: The History of Sexuality I*. London: Penguin Books.

Foucault, Michel (1991). *Discipline and Punishment: The Birth of the Prison*. London: Penguin Books.

Foucault, Michel (1978/1976). *History of Sexuality*, vol. 1. New York: Pantheon Books.

Freud, Sigmund (1977). *On Sexuality: Three Essays on the Theory of Sexuality and Other Works*. Richards, Angela (ed.). London: Penguin Books.

Frosh, Stephen (1999). *The Politics of Psychoanalysis*. London: Macmillan.

Frosh, Stephen (1995). 'Time, space and otherness', pp. 291–308. In Pile, Steve and Thrift, Nigel (eds). *Mapping the Subject: Geographies of Cultural Transformation*. London: Routledge.

Gamman, Lorraine and Makinen, Merja (1994). *Female Fetishism: A New Look*. London: Lawrence & Wishart.

Ghatak, Saran (2010). '"The Opium Wars": the biopolitics of narcotic control in the United States, 1914–1935'. *Critical Criminology*, vol. 18, pp. 41–56.

Gianesi, Ana Paula Lacorte (2002). *Toxicômano? Considerações Psicanalíticas sobre a Toxicomania, o Objeto Droga e o Sujeito da Psicanálise*. São Paulo: Master thesis defended in the Faculty of Psychology of the University of São Paulo (USP).

Gilroy, Paul (2000). *Between Camps: Race, Identity and Nationalism at the End of the Colour Line*. Harmondsworth: Allen Lane.

Goffman, Erving (1963). *Stigma*. London: Penguin.

Goldberg, Ted (1999). *Demystifying Drugs: A Psychosocial Perspective*. London: Macmillan.

Goodman, Jordan, Lovejoy, Paul and Sherratt, Andrew (1995). *Consuming Habits: Drugs in History and Anthropology*. London: Routledge.

Gordo-López, Ángel (2002). 'El estado actual de la psicología crítica'. *Athenea Digital*, vol. 1, pp. 1–9.

Gordo-López, Ángel and Linaza, J. L. (eds) (1996). *Psicologías, Discursos y Poder*. Madrid: Visor.

Gostin, Lawrence (1997). 'The legal regulation of smoking (and smokers): public health or secular morality?', pp. 331–357. In Brandt, Allan M. and Rozin, Paul (eds). *Morality and Health*. London: Routledge.

Grosz, Elizabeth (1990). *Jacques Lacan: A Feminist Introduction*. London: Routledge.

Gurfinkel, Decio (1996). 'A droga e a coisa: sobre a delimitação do conceito de toxicomania', pp. 225–238. In Cohen, C., Ferraz, F.C. and Segre, M. (eds). *Saúde Mental, Crime e Justiça*. São Paulo: Edusp.

Gusfield, Joseph (1997). 'The culture of public problems: drinking-driving and the symbolic order', pp. 201–229. In Brandt, Allan M. and Rozin, Paul (eds). *Morality and Health*. London: Routledge.

Hall, Stuart (2008). *Da Diáspora: Identidades e Mediações Culturais*. Belo Horizonte: Editora UFMG.

Haaken, Janice (2002). 'Bitch and fem psychology: women, aggression and psychoanalytic social theory'. *Journal for the Psychoanalysis of Culture and Society*, vol. 7, no. 2. pp. 202–215.

Haraway, Donna (1996). 'Situated knowledges: the science question in feminism and the privilege of partial perspective', pp. 249–263. In Keller, Evelyn Fox and Longino, Helen (eds). *Feminism and Science: Oxford Readings in Feminism*. Oxford: Oxford University Press.

Harding, Sandra (1996). 'Rethinking standpoint epistemology: what is "strong objectivity"?', pp. 235–248. In Keller, Evelyn Fox and Longino, Helen (eds). *Feminism and Science: Oxford Readings in Feminism*. Oxford: Oxford University Press.

Harding, Sandra (1986). 'Is there a feminist method?', pp. 1–14. In Harding, Sandra (ed.). *Feminism and Methodology*. Buckingham: Open University Press.

Harm Reduction International (IHRA) (2010). Retrieved in 2010 from www.ihra.net/history.

Harm Reduction International (2011). History. Retrieved in 2011 from www.ihra.net/history.

Harper, Rosalynn, Harper, Gemma and Stockdale, Janet (2002). 'The role and sentencing of women in drug trafficking crime'. *Legal and Criminological Psychology*, vol. 7, pp. 101–114, February.

Harrison, Brian (1971). *Drink and the Victorians: The Temperance Question in England 1815–1972*. London: Faber & Faber.

Healy, David (2004). *Let Them Eat Prozac: The Unhealthy Relationship between the Pharmaceutical Industry and Depression*. New York: New York University Press.

Healy, David (1997). *The Anti-Depressant Era*. Cambridge, MA: Harvard University Press.

Heath, Dwight (1987). 'A decade of development in the anthropological study of alcohol use, 1970–1980', pp. 16–69. In Douglas, Mary (ed.). *Constructive Drinking: Perspectives on Drink from Anthropology*. Cambridge: Cambridge University Press.

Heidegger, Martin (1997). *Being and Time*. Oxford: Blackwell.

Henderson, Sheila (1999). 'Drugs and culture: the question of gender', pp. 36–48. In South, Nigel (ed.). *Drugs: Cultures, Controls and Everyday Life*. London: Sage.

Herzberg, David Lowell (2009). *Happy Pills in America: From Miltown to Prozac*. Baltimore, MD: John Hopkins University Press.

Hickman, Timothy A. (2000). 'Drugs and race in American culture: Orientalism in the turn-of-the-century discourse of narcotic addiction'. *American Studies*, vol. 41, no. 1, pp. 71–91.

Hoare, Jacqueline and Moon, Debbie (eds) (2010). *Drug Misuse Declared: Findings from the 2009/10*. British Crime Survey, England and Wales. Home Office statistical bulletin.

Hockey, Jenny (1993). 'Women and health', pp. 250–271. In Richardson, Diane and Robinson, Victoria (eds). *Introducing Women's Studies*. London: Macmillan.

Hook, Derek (2012). *A Critical Psychology of the Postcolonial: The Mind of Apartheid*. London: Routledge.

hooks, bell (2000). *Feminist Theory: From Margin to Centre*. London: Pluto Press.

Hugh-Jones, Stephen (1995). 'Coca, beer, cigars and yage: meals and anti-meals in an Ameridian community', pp. 47–67. In Goodman, Jordan, Lovejoy, Paul and Sherratt, Andrew (eds). *Consuming Habits: Drugs in History and Anthropology*. London: Routledge.

Hunt, Neil and Stevens, Alex (2004). 'Whose harm? Harm reduction and the shift to coercion in UK drug policy'. *Social Policy & Society*, vol. 3, no. 4, pp. 333–342.

Illich, Ivan (1995). *Limits to Medicine: Medical Nemesis: The Exploration of Health*. London: Marion Boyars.

Inciardi, James and Harrison, Lana (2000). *Harm Reduction: National and International Perspectives*. London: Sage.

Irigaray, Luce (1989). 'The gesture in psychoanalysis', pp. 127–138. In Brennan, T. (ed.). *Between Feminism and Psychoanalysis*. London: Routledge.

Jacobson, Bobbie (1986). *Beating the LadyKillers: Women and Smoking*. London: Pluto Press.

Jacobson, Bobbie (1981). *The LadyKillers: Why Smoking is a Feminist Issue*. London: Pluto Press.

Karam, Maria Lucia (2008). 'A lei 11.343/06 e os repetidos danos do proibicionismo', pp. 105–122. In Labate, Beatriz C., Goulart, Sandra, Fiore, Mauricio, MacRae, Edward and Carneiro, Henrique (eds). *Drogas e Cultura: Novas Perspectivas*. Salvador: EDUFBA.

Karsten, Carien (1993). *Female Hard Drug-Users in Crisis: Childhood Traumas and Survival Strategies*. Book available at www.drugtext.com.

Katz, Solomon (1997). 'Secular morality', pp. 297–330. In Brandt, Allan and Rozin, Paul (eds). *Morality and Health*. London: Routledge.

Keane, Helen (1999). 'Adventures of the addicted brain'. *Australian Feminist Studies*, vol. 14, no. 29, pp. 63–76.

Keane, Helen, Moore, David and Fraser, Susanne (2011). 'Addiction and dependence: making realities in the DSM'. *Addiction*, vol. 106, no. 5, pp. 875–877.

Keire, Mara L. (1998). 'Dope fiends and degenerates: the gendering of addiction in the early twentieth century'. *Journal of Social History*, vol. 31, no. 4, pp. 809–822.

Kendall, Gavin and Wickham, Gary (1999). *Using Foucault's Methods: Introducing Qualitative Methods*. London: Sage Publications.

Klee, Hilary (2002). 'Women, family and drugs', pp. 3–14. In Klee, Hilary, Jackson, Marcia and Lewis, Susan (eds) *Drug Misuse and Motherhood*. London: Routledge.

Klee, Hilary, Jackson, Marcia and Lewis, Susan (eds) (2002). *Drug Misuse and Motherhood*. London: Routledge.

Klein, Richard (1995). *Cigarettes are Sublime*. London: Picador Press.

Kohn, Marek (1992). *Dope Girls: The Birth of the British Underground*. London: Lawrence and Wishart.

Kristeva, Julia (1982). *Powers of Horror: An Essay on Abjection*. New York: Columbia University Press.

Labate, Beatriz C., Goulart, Sandra, Fiore, Mauricio, MacRae, Edward and Carneiro, Henrique (2008). *Drogas e Cultura: Novas Perspectivas*. Salvador: EDUFBA.

Laboratory and Scientific Section United Nations Office on Drugs and Crime (2003). *Terminology and Information on Drugs*. Second edition. New York: United Nations.

Labrousse, Alain (2010). *Geopolítica das Drogas*. São Paulo: Desatino.

Lacan, Jacques (1995). *A Relação de Objeto: Livro 4*. Rio de Janeiro: Jorge Zahar.

Lacan, Jacques (1994). *Four Fundamental Concepts of Psycho-Analysis*. London: Penguin.

Lacan, Jacques (1991). *The Seminar of Jacques Lacan. Book I: Freud's Papers on Techniques – 1953–1954*. In Miller, Jacques-Alain (ed.). London: W.W. Norton & Company.

Lacan, Jacques (1989). *Écrits: A Selection*. London: Tavistock/Routledge.

Lenson, David (1995). *On Drugs*. Minneapolis, MN: University of Minnesota Press.

Lewis, Susan (2002). 'Concepts of motherhood', pp. 32–44. In Klee, Hilary, Jackson, Marcia and Lewis, Susan (eds). *Drug Misuse and Motherhood*. London: Routledge.

Littlewood, Roland (1994). 'Symptoms, Struggles and Functions: What does the Overdose Represent?', pp. 79–97. In McDonald, Maryon (ed.). *Gender, Drink and Drugs*. Oxford: Berg.

Littlewood, Roland and Lipsedge, Maurice (1989). *Aliens and Alienists: Ethnic Minorities and Psychiatry*. London: Unwin Hyman Ltd.

Lloyd, Charlie (2010). *Sinning and Sinned Against: The Stigmatisation of Problem Drug Users*. London: UK Drug Policy Commission.

Longino, Helen (2009). 'Can there be a feminist science?', pp. 210–217. In Cudd, Anne E. and Andreasen, Robin O. (eds). *Feminist Theory: A Philosophical Anthology*. Oxford: Blackwell.

Loose, Rik (2002a). *The Subject of Addiction: Psychoanalysis and the Administration of Enjoyment*. London: Karnac.

Loose, Rik (2002b). 'A Lacanian approach to clinical diagnosis and addiction', pp. 263–289. In Glynos and Stavrakakis (eds). *Lacan and Science*. London: Karnac.

Lopes, Ruth Gelehrter C. (1999). *As Interpretações Sociais da Saúde na Velhice, Refletidas no Uso do Medicamento*. Doctorate research defended at the Faculty of Health Care Studies at the University de São Paulo, USP.

Lunbeck, Elizabeth (1994). *The Psychiatric Persuasion: Knowledge, Gender and Power in Modern America*. Princeton, NJ: Princeton University Press.

Macey, David (1995). 'On the subject of Lacan', pp. 72–86. In Elliott, Anthony and Frosh, Stephen (eds). *Paths Between Theory and Modern Culture: Psychoanalysis in Contexts*. London: Routledge.

MacGregor, Susanne (1999). 'Medicine, custom or moral fibre: policy responses to drug misuse', pp. 67–85. In South, Nigel (ed.). *Drugs: Cultures, Controls and Everyday Life*. London: Sage.

Machado, Ana Regina and Miranda, Paulo Sérgio Carneiro (2007). 'Fragmentos da história da atenção à saúde para usuários de alcool e outras drogas no Brasil: da Justiça à Saúde Pública'. *História, Ciências, Saúde: Manguinhos*, Rio de Janeiro, vol. 14, no. 3, pp. 801–821.

MacRae, Edward (1998). *Santo Daime and Santa Maria: The Licit Ritual Use of Ayahuasca and the Illicit Use of Cannabis in a Brazilian Amazonian Religion. International Journal of Drug Policy*, vol. 9, pp. 325–338.

Marks, Deb (1996). 'Constructing a narrative: moral discourse and Young's people experiences of exclusion', pp. 114–130. In Burman, Erica, Aitken, Gill, Alldred, Pam, Allwood, Robin, Billington, Tom, Goldberg, Brenda, Gordo-López, Angel, Heenan, Colleen, Marks, Deborah and Warner, Sam (eds). *Psychology Discourse Practice: From Regulation to Resistance*. London: Taylor & Francis.

Marx, Karl (1990). *Capital*, vol. 1. London: Penguin Books.

Masur, Jandira and Carlini, Elisaldo Luís (1993). *Drogas: Subsídios para uma Discussão*. São Paulo: Editora Brasiliense.

Maynard, Mary (1994). 'Methods, practice and epistemology: the debate about feminism and research', pp. 10–27. In Mary Maynard and June Purvis (eds). *Researching Women's Lives from a Feminism Perspective*. London: Taylor & Francis.

Maugh, Thomas H. (2010). 'Cigarettes to carry grim warnings'. *Los Angeles Times*. Accessed in November 2010. www.articles.latimes.com/2010/nov/11/science/la-sci-1111-cigarette-packages-20101111.

McClintock, Anne (1995). *Imperial Leather: Race, Gender and Sexuality in the Colonial Contest*. London: Routledge.

McDonald, Maryon (1994). *Gender, Drink and Drugs*. Oxford: Berg.

McKenna, Terence (1992). *Food of the Gods: The Search for the Original Tree of Knowledge. A Radical History of Plants, Drugs and Human Evolution*. London: Rider Publications.

McMurran, Mary (1994). *The Psychology of Addiction*. London: Taylor & Francis.

McSweeney, Tim, Stevens, Alex, Hunt, Neil and Turnbull, Paul (2006). 'Twisting arms or a helping hand? Assessing the impact of "coerced" and comparable "voluntary" drug treatment options'. *British Journal of Criminology*, pp. 1–21.

McSweeney, Tim, Turnbull, Paul J. and Hough, Mike (2008). *Tackling Drug Markets and Distribution Networks in the UK: A Review of the Recent Literature*. Institute for Criminal Policy Research. London: UK Drug Policy Commission.

Medicines Act (1968). www.legislation.gov.uk/ukpga/1968/67/contents.

Misuse of Drugs Act (1971). www.legislation.gov.uk/uksi/2005/3178/contents/made.

Moi, Toril (2010). *Sexual/Textual Politics*. London: Routledge.

Moncrieff, Joanna (2008). 'The creation of the concept of an antidepressant: An historical analysis'. *Social Science & Medicine*, vol. 66, pp. 2346–2355.

Moore, Michael, Yuen, Ho Ming, Dunn, Nick, Mullee, Mark A., Maskell, Joe and Kendrick, Tony (2009). 'Explaining the rise in antidepressant prescribing: a descriptive study using the general practice research database'. *BMJ*, pp. 1–7.

Mountian, Ilana (2009). 'Social imaginary for critical research'. In Owens, Carol (ed.), 'Psychoanalysis'. *Annual Review of Critical Psychology*, issue 6, pp. 205–222.

Mountian, Ilana (2007). 'Mujeres bajo control', pp. 73–83. In Biglia, B. and San Martín, C. (eds). *Estado de Wonderbra. Entretejiendo Narrativas de Feministas Sobre las Violencias de Género*. Barcelona: Virus Press.

Mountian, Ilana (2006). 'Identifying the enemy: deconstructing drugs and addiction', pp. 135–151. In Myers, William (ed.). *The Range of Evil: Multi-disciplinary Studies of Human Wickedness*, vol. 26. Oxford: Interdisciplinary Press.

Mountian, Ilana (2005a). 'Images of women and drugs'. In Zavos, A., Biglia, B., Clark, J. and Motzkau, J. (eds). 'Feminisms and activisms'. *Annual Review of Critical Psychology*, issue 4, pp. 81–95.

Mountian, Ilana (2005b). *Young Asylum Seekers, Refugees and Drug Use: Research Report*. Manchester: Manchester Metropolitan University and Early Break.

Mountian, Ilana (2004a). *Drugs, Gender and Social Imaginary*. Doctoral research thesis. Manchester: Manchester Metropolitan University.

Mountian, Ilana (2004b). Article: 'Questões Éticas e Morais do Conceito de Drogadição'. In online journal *Portal da Psicologia*, Portugal.

Mountian, Ilana (1999). *Drug Misuse and the Perspective of Future*. Masters research thesis. ALFA programme. Manchester: Manchester Metropolitan University.

Mountian, Ilana and Calvo Gonzalez, Elena (2012). 'Race, class and affirmative action in Brazil: reflections from a feminist perspective'. *Feminism & Psychology*, vol. 22, no. 2, pp. 240–248.

Mountian, Ilana and Lara Jr, Nadir (2010). 'Psicologia e cultura: conceituações e debates', pp. 165–197. In Alves, Paulo César (ed.). *Cultura: Múltiplas Leituras*. Bauru: EDUSC; Salvador: EDUFBA.

Mountian, Ilana, Lawthom, Rebecca, Kellock, Anne, Duggan, Karen, Sixsmith, Judith, Kagan, Carolyn, Hawkins, Jennifer, Haworth, John, Siddiquee, Asiya, Worley, Claire, Brown, David, Griffiths John and Purcell, Christina (eds) (2011). 'On utilising a visual methodology: shared reflections and tensions'. In Reavey, Paula (ed.). *Visual Psychologies: Using and Interpreting Images in Qualitative Research*. London: Routledge.

Murji, Karim (1999). 'White lines: culture, "race" and drugs', pp. 49–65. In South, Nigel (ed.). *Drugs: Cultures, Controls and Everyday Life*. London: Sage.

Murphy, Sheigla and Rosenbaum, Marsha (1999). *Pregnant Women on Drugs: Combating Stereotypes and Stigma*. Brunswick, NJ: Rutgers University Press.

Musto, David F. (1999). *The American Disease: Origins of Narcotic Control*. Oxford: Oxford University Press.

Neill, Calum (2011). *Lacanian Ethics and the Assumption of Subjectivity*. Basingstoke: Palgrave Macmillan.

Nieves, Otomie Vale (1994). 'Lo entre-dicho del discurso lacaniano con respecto a la subjectividad de las mujeres', pp. 70–91. In Figueroa-Sarriera, Heidi, López, María Milagros and Roman, Madeline (eds). *Mas Alla de la Bella (In) Diferencia: Revision Post-Feminista y Otras Escrituras Posibles*. San Juan: Publicaciones Puertoriqueñas.

O'Bryan, Lee (1989). 'Young people and drugs', pp. 64–75. In MacGregor, Susanne (ed.). *Drugs and British Society: Responses to a Social Problem in the Eighties*. London: Routledge.
Oakley, Ann (1981). *Interviewing Women: A Contradiction in Terms*. In Roberts, H. (ed.). *Doing Feminist Research*. London: Routledge.
Oenen, Gijs van (2000a). *Looking Awry Setting Law Straight. How to Take Care of Legal Trauma*. Rotterdam: Department of Philosophy, Erasmus University Rotterdam.
Oenen, Gijs van (2000b). *Citizenship and 'Informal Rule of Law'. How Lax Enforcement can Sustain the Rule of Law*. Rotterdam: Dept of Philosophy, Erasmus University Rotterdam.
Olievenstein, Claude (ed.) (1989). *A Clínica do Toxicômano: A Falta da Falta*. Porto Alegre: Artes Médicas.
Osborne, Thomas (1994). 'On anti-medicine and clinical reason', pp. 28–47. In Jones, Colin and Porter, Roy (eds). *Reassessing Foucault: Power, Medicine and the Body*. London: Routledge.
Padayachee, Anshu (1998). 'The hidden health burden: alcohol-abusing women, misunderstood and mistreat'. *International Journal of Drug Policy*, vol. 9, no. 1, February, pp. 57–62.
Palmary, Ingrid, Burman, Erica, Chantler, Khatidja and Kiguwa, Peace (2010). *Gender and Migration: Feminist Interventions*. London: Zed Books.
Parascandola, John (1996). 'The drug habit: the association of the word "drug" with abuse in American history', pp. 156–167. In Potter, Roy and Teich, Mikulas (eds). *Drugs and Narcotics in History*. Cambridge: Cambridge University Press.
Parker, Ian (2011). *Lacanian Psychoanalysis: Revolutions in Subjectivity*. London: Routledge.
Parker, Ian (2007). *Revolution in Psychology: Alienation to Emancipation*. London: Pluto Press.
Parker, Ian (2002). *Discursive Resources in Discourse Unit*. In Discourse Analysis Online. Retrieved from www.shu.ac.uk/daol (accessed June 2012).
Parker, Ian (1997). *Psychoanalytic Culture: Psychoanalytic Discourse in Western Society*. London: Sage.
Parker, Ian (1992). *Discourse Dynamics: Critical Analysis for Social and Individual Psychology*. London: Routledge.
Pateman, Carole (1988). *The Sexual Contract*. Stanford, CA: Stanford University Press.
Phillips, Anne (2010). *Gender and Culture*. Cambridge: Polity Press.
Plant, Sadie (1999). *Writing on Drugs*. London: Faber & Faber.
Prado, Marco Aurélio Máximo, Mountian, Ilana, Machado, Frederico Viana and Santos, Leonel Cardoso (2010). 'Los movimientos LGTB y la lucha por la democratización de las jerarquias sexuales en Brasil'. Mexico: *Revista Digital Universitaria*, vol. 11, no. 7, pp. 1–15. www.revista.unam.mx/vol.11/num7/art68/index.html.

Prado, Marco Aurélio Máximo and Machado, Frederico Viana (2008). *Preconceito Contra Homosexualidades: A Hierarquia da Invisivilidade*. São Paulo: Cortez editora.

Project Provention.org (2010). www.projectprevention.org.

Pulp Magazine (2003). 'Are you a slob?', Manchester: Manchester Student Magazine.

Radcliffe, Polly and Stevens, A. (2008). 'Are drug treatment services only for 'thieving junkie scumbags'? Drug users and the management of stigmatised identities'. *Social Science & Medicine* 67, pp. 1065–1073.

Raine, Pamela (2001). *Women's Perspectives on Drugs and Alcohol: The Vicious Circle*. Aldershot: Ashgate.

Reuter, Peter (2011). *Options for Regulating New Psychoactive Drugs: A Review of Recent Experiences*. London: UK Drug Policy Commission.

Reuter, Peter and Stevens, Alex (2007). *An Analysis of UK Drug Policy: A Monograph*, London: UK Drug Policy Commission. Retrieved in 2012 from www.ukdpc.org.uk.

Rodrigues, Thiago (2004). *Política e Drogas nas Américas*. São Paulo: EDUC.

Rodrigues, Thiago (2003). *Narcotráfico: Uma Guerra na Guerra*. São Paulo: Desatino.

Rohden, Fabiola (2003). 'The construction of sexual difference in medicine'. *Caderno Saúde Pública*, vol. 19, pp. 201–212.

Rosa, Miriam Debieux (2000). *Histórias que não se Contam: O Não-Dito e a Psicanálise com Crianças e Adolescentes*. São Paulo: Cabral Editora Universitária

Rosa, Miriam Debieux (1999). 'A subjectivação nas configurações familiares da "pós-modernidade"', pp. 79–104. In *Psicanálise e Universidade*. São Paulo: numbers 9 and 10, PUC/S.P.

Rosa, Miriam Debieux (1999a). 'A subjectivação nas configurações familiares da "pós-modernidade"', pp. 79–104. In *Psicanálise e Universidade de São Paulo*, nos. 9 and 10. PUC/SP.

Rosa, Miriam Debieux (1999b). 'O discurso e o ato na produção do laço social: reflexões sobre a delinqüência', pp. 275–287. In *Congresso Internacional de Psicanalise e suas Conexões: Trata-se Uma Criança*. Rio de Janeiro: Companhia de Freud, vol. 1, pp. 275–287.

Rosa, Miriam Debieux and Mountian, Ilana (2012). 'Psychoanalytic listening of socially excluded young people'. *Psychoanalysis, Culture and Society*. Hampshire: Palgrave.

Rose, Jacqueline (1994). Femininity and its discontents', pp. 42–53. In Evans, Mary (ed.). *The Woman Question*. London: Sage.

Rose, Nikolas (1994). 'Medicine, history and the present', pp. 25–47. In Jones, Colin and Porter, Roy (eds). *Reassessing Foucault: Power, Medicine and the Body*. London: Rotuledge.

Royal College of Psychiatrists (2000). *Dilemmas and Choices*. London: Royal College of Psychiatrists.

Ruggiero, Vincenzo (1999). 'Drug as a password and the law as a drug: discussing the legalisation of illicit substances', pp. 123–137. In South, Nigel (ed.). *Drugs: Cultures, Controls and Everyday Life*. London: Sage.

Saussure, Ferdinand de (1974). *Course in General Linguistics*. London: Peter Owen.

Scheidlinger, Saul (1982). 'Residential address: on scapegoating in group psychotherapy'. *International Journal of Psychology*, vol. 32, pp. 131–142.

Sedgwick, Eve Kosofsky (1992). 'Epidemics of the will', pp. 582–595. In Crary, Jonathan and Kwinter, Sanford (eds). *Incorporations*. New York: Zone.

Sedgwick, Eve Kosofsky (1991). *Epistemology of the Closet*. Los Angeles, CA: University of California Press.

Shapiro, Harry (1999). 'Dances with drugs: pop music, drugs and youth culture', pp. 17–35. In South, Nigel (ed.) *Drugs: Cultures, Controls and Everyday Life*. London: Sage.

Singleton, Nicola (2010). *Attitudes to Drug Dependence Results from a Survey of People Living in Private Households in the UK*. London: UK Drug Policy Commission.

Silva, Tomaz Tadeu, Hall, Stuart and Woodward, Kathryn (2000). *Identidade e Diferença: A Perspectiva dos Estudos Culturais*. Petrópolis: Editora Vozes.

Spandler, Helen and Bastleer, Janet (2000). 'Sparring partners: conflicts in the expression and treatment of self-harm'. In Bastller, Janet and Humphries, Beth (eds). *Welfare, Exclusion and Political Agency*. London: Routledge.

Spivak, Gayatri Chakravorty (1988). 'Can the subaltern speak?', pp. 271–313. In Nelson, C. and Grossberg, L. (eds). *Marxism and the Interpretation of Culture*. Basingstoke: Macmillan.

Stacey, Jackie (1993). 'Untangling feminist theory', pp. 49–73. In Richardson, Diane and Robinson, Victoria (eds). *Introducing Women's Studies*. London: Macmillan.

Stanley, Liz and Wise, Sue (eds) (1990). *Method, Methodology and Epistemology in Feminist Research Processes in Feminist Praxis*. London: Routledge.

Stimson, Gerry (2000). 'Blair declares war: the unhealthy state of British drug policy', *The International Journal of Drug Policy*, 11, 259–264.

Stimson, Gerry (1994). 'Can a war on drugs succeed?', pp. 313–318. In Coomber, Ross (ed.). *Drugs and Drug Use in Society: A Critical Reader*. Kent: Greenwich Press.

South, Nigel (1999). 'Debating drugs and everyday life: normalisation, prohibition and "otherness"', pp. 1–16. In South, Nigel (ed.). *Drugs: Cultures, Controls and Everyday Life*. London: Sage.

South, Nigel (1994). 'Voices from the past: drugs and social history – from Virginia Berridge to Marek Kohn'. In *IJDP Ltd.*, vol 5, no. 4. Available at www.drugtext.org/articles/945412.html.

Szasz, Thomas (1994). 'The ethics of addiction', pp. 373–382. In Coomber, Ross (ed.). *Drugs and Drug Use in Society: A Critical Reader*. Kent: Greenwich University Press.

Szasz, Thomas (1975). *Ceremonial Chemistry: The Ritual Persecution of Drugs, Addicts, and Pushers*. London: Routledge & Kegan Paul.

Taylor, F. and Rey, J. (1953). 'The scapegoat motif in society and its manifestations in a therapeutic group'. *International Journal of Psychoanalysis*, vol. 34, pp. 253–264.

Teo, Thomas (2005). *The Critique of Psychology: From Kant to Post-colonial Theory*. New York: Springer.

Tracy, Sarah W. and Acker, Caroline Jean (2004). *Altering American Consciousness: The History of Alcohol and Drug Abuse in the United States, 1800–2000*. Amhurst, MA: University of Massachusetts Press.

United Nations Commission on Narcotic Drugs (2010). Report on the fifty-third session, New York: Economic and Social Council. Available at: www.unodc.org/documents/commissions/CND-Uploads/CND-53-RelatedFiles/E2010_28eV1052082.pdf.

United Nations Office on Drugs and Crime (2003). Terminology and information on drugs. New York: United Nations Office on Drugs and Crime. ISBN: 92-1-148163-5. Retrieved in 2012 from www.unodc.org/unodc/en/scientists/terminology-and-information-on-drugs.html.

Ussher, Jane (1998). 'A feminist perspective', pp. 150–161. In Velleman, Richard, Copello, Alex and Maslin, Jenny (eds). *Living With Drink: Women Who Live With Problem Drinkers*. London: Longman.

Vargas, Eduardo Viana (2008). 'Fármacos eoutros objetos sócio-técnicos: notas para uma genealogia das drogas', pp. 41–65. In Labate, Beatriz C., Goulart, Sandra, Fiore, Mauricio, MacRae, Edward and Carneiro, Henrique (eds). *Drogas e Cultura: Novas Perspectivas*. Salvador: EDUFBA.

Velleman, Richard, Copello, Alex and Maslin, Jenny (eds) (1998). *Living With Drink: Women Who Live With Problem Drinkers*. London: Longman.

Von Zuben, Newton Aquiles (1984). 'Fenomenologia e existência: uma leitura de Merleau Ponty'. In Martins, Joel and Dichtchekenian, Maria Fernanda (eds). *Temas Fundamentais da Fenomenologia*. Centro de Estudos Fenomenológicos de São Paulo. São Paulo: Editora Moraes.

Walkerdine, Valerie (1997). *Daddy's Girl: Young Girls and Popular Culture*. Basingstoke: Macmillan.

Walton, James (2000). *The Faber Book of Smoking*. London: Faber & Faber.

Warner, Michael (1999). *The Trouble with Normal: Sex, Politics, and the Ethics of Queer Life*. Cambridge, MA: Harvard University Press.

Warner, Sam (1996). 'Women and high security mental hospitals', pp. 96–113. In Burman, Erica, Aitken, Gill, Alldred, Pam, Allwood, Robin, Billington, Tom, Goldberg, Brenda, Gordo-López, Angel, Heenan, Colleen, Marks, Deborah and Warner, Sam (eds). *Psychology Discourse Practice: From Regulation to Resistance*. London: Taylor & Francis.

White, William L. (2004). 'Lessons of language: historical perspectives on the rethoric of addiction', pp. 33–60. In Tracy, Sarah W. and Acker, Caroline Jean (eds). *Altering American Consciousness: The History of Alcohol and Drug Abuse in the United States, 1800–2000*. Minneapolis, MN: University of Minnesota Press.

Wittgenstein, Ludwig (1968). *Philosophical Investigations*. Oxford: Blackwell.

Wright, Samantha (2002). 'Women's use of drugs: gender specific factors' pp. 15–31. In Klee, Hilary, Jackson, Marcia and Lewis, Susan (eds). *Drug Misuse and Motherhood*. London: Routledge.

Xiberras, Martine (1989). *A Sociedade Intoxicada*. Lisbon: Instituto Piaget.

Young, Jock (1971). *The Drugtakers: The Social Meaning of Drug users*. London: Granada Publishing.

Young, Malcolm (1994). 'The police, gender and the culture of drug use and addiction', pp. 55–75. In McDonald, Maryon (ed.). *Gender, Drink and Drugs*. Oxford: Berg.

Yuval-Davis, Nira (1997). *Gender & Nation*. London: Sage.

Wilde, Oscar (2007/1892). *Lady Windermere's Fan*. London: Penguin.

World Health Organisation (WHO) (1994). *Lexicon of Alcohol and Drug Terms*. Geneva: World Health Organisation. Retrieved in 2011 from http://whqlibdoc.who.int/publications/9241544686.pdf.

Zieger, Susan Marjorie (2008). *Inventing the Addict: Drugs, Race and Sexuality in Nineteenth Century in British and American Literature*. Minneapolis, MN: University of Minnesota Press.

Zinberg, Norman (1984). *Drug, Set, and Setting: The Basis for Controlled Intoxicant Use*. New Haven, CT: Yale University Press.

Žižek, Slavoj (1998). 'Love thy neighbour. No thanks'. In Lane, C. (ed.). *The Psychoanalysis of Race*. New York: Columbia University Press.

Žižek, Slavoj (1992). *Enjoy Your Symptom! Jacques Lacan in Hollywood and Out*. London: Routledge.

Zoja, Luigi (1989). *Drugs, Addiction and Initiation: The Modern Search for Ritual*. Boston, MA: Sigo Press.

Index

Locators in *italics* indicate pages with illustrations.